Milton Today

Milton Today

M.V. Rama Sarma

PRESTIGE

Published by
PRESTIGE BOOKS
3/28, East Patel Nagar
New Delhi 110 008

ISBN: 81-7551-093-5

Composed by Vivek Mathur, Delhi 110 006 Ph. 3981867
Printed at Chaman Offset Press, New Delhi 110 002

Contents

Preface

Milton Today presents Milton as the champion of the good old cause, the Grand Whig, the exponent of justice in God's ways, the staunch advocate of his native language, English, and as the upholder of the cross-cultural assimilation of the east and the west. In pleading for the cause of the Commonwealth and in fighting for individual freedom Milton becomes the contemporary of every age. His vision of a millennium, a golden age of golden deeds, acquires a universality of its own.

Milton Today is an innovative attempt to bring together Milton's contribution to the cause of liberty and his unflinching faith in God's justice. It is a rewarding experience to visualise Milton's catholicity of outlook in trying to establish a new world order 'founded in righteousness and peace and love.'

Tirupati **M.V. RAMA SARMA**

The Good Old Cause

Milton reveals himself as a poet of a serious mould even while he is a student at Cambridge. In his poem *At a Vacation Exercise* written in 1627, in his nineteenth year, he says that he will choose 'a graver subject' and not opt for "the new fangled toys" of "the late fantastics." Later in 1629 he writes *The Nativity Ode* at the age of twenty-one, still a student at Cambridge and it shows that he has come of age as a poet. In his letter to his friend, Charles Diodati (1629) he states, "I am writing a poem about the king who was born of heavenly seed, and who brought peace to man. I am writing about the blessed ages promised in the Holy Scriptures. . . . These are the gifts I have given for Christ's birthday, the first light of the dawn brought them to me."

Apparently this poem refers to *The Nativity Ode*, the first major English poem that Milton writes on the Christmas morning. In *The Nativity Ode* Milton uses "the idea of sacred poetry as a gift, a consecration." (Broadbent, 101) He considers himself to be a poet sacred to the gods, and he is a poet with a purpose. *The Nativity Ode* clearly introduces the two ideas, of a golden age of golden deeds, and of a contemplative type of hero like Christ in the human form. These novel ideas sound like a prophetic strain for they repeat themselves in the three long poems written towards the close of his life.

Milton associates the poet's mission with high seriousness. He thinks that a poet longing for immortality should live "frugally" on a "harmless diet" like "herbs." In the *Sixth Elegy* addressed to Charles Diodati (1629) he says that "the poet's youth must be chaste, and free from crime, his morals strict and his hand unstained." The poet has to lead a sublime life. Again in his letter to Charles Diodati in 1637, he says that he is growing his wings and meditating flight, but as yet the 'Pegasus raises himself on very tender pinions.' In his *Apology for Smeetymnus* (1641) Milton states again that 'he who would not be frustrate of his hope to write well hereafter in laudable things, ought himself to be a true poem, that is, a composition and pattern of the best and honourablest things.' The poet has to lead an exemplary life, and great poetry is 'the inspired gift of God, rarely bestowed.' Such poets, though rare, are commissioned by God 'to imbreed and cherish in a great people the seeds of virtue and public civility.' Also they have 'to celebrate in glorious and lofty hymns the throne and equipage of God's almightiness' (*The Reason of Church Government*). Milton feels that the poet has an obligation to society and he has to be a priest celebrating the glory of God in lofty hymns. He thinks that the function of the poet is that of the prophet in the Old dispensation. It is God's truth that he has to utter. Milton combines within himself 'the roles of teacher, orator, priest and especially the Hebrew prophet.' (Broadbent, 86) He sees himself 'as one of a line of prophets of whom Christ was the greatest.' (Hill, 357) He wants to write a great poem 'doctrinal and exemplary to a nation.' In *The Reason of Church Government* Milton assures the knowing reader that he will give a work, 'not to be raised from the heat of youth, or the vapours of wine, like that which flows at waste from the pen of a rhyming parasite.' It will be a noble poem that posterity may not 'willingly let it die.'

In order to write his great poems Milton wants to have comprehensive knowledge. So after taking his M.A. Degree from Cambridge he stays with his parents for six years, 1632-38, at Hammersmith and Horton, reading on his own, books of travel, history and geography. This is also the period when he writes the minor poems, *L'Allegro, Il Penseroso, Comus* and *Lycidas*. Milton plans to have a personal knowledge of European culture, if possible oriental culture also. He starts on his Italian journey in 1638, but after fifteen months he returns to London for he hears that civil war is about to start in England. During his stay in Italy he actively participates in the intellectual and religious discussions in the academies.

On his return he plans to write a national epic. But his hasty marriage with Mary Powell in 1642 results in his writing the divorce pamphlets, pleading for divorce when there is incompatibility of temperament between husband and wife. Milton's essential love for individual liberty and freedom of the nation leads him to the questioning of the domestic, religious, and political practices of his day. He believes solemnly that England is blessed by God for the English people have been fighting for freedom and ruthlessly opposing the divine right theory of kingship of Charles I. For nearly twenty years, 1640-1660, Milton involves himself in the prose pamphleteering work. It may be said that 'no English writer in any age has ever pressed his faith in England with more impassioned ardour and greater eloquence than Milton.' (Hutchinson, 90) When he expresses his faith in England 'he speaks as a Hebrew Prophet would speak of the Chosen Race' (*Ibid*). He writes as a prophet with self-confidence and awareness of a greater destiny for his nation. Especially his two prose tracts *Areopagitica* and *On Education* read like 'documents of a prophetic rather than a purely practical character.' (Grierson, 54) Milton triumphantly pleads in *Areopagitica*, 'Give me the liberty to know, to utter, and to argue freely according to conscience, above all liberties.' He thinks 'God's Englishmen' will establish a new world order where justice prevails, truth operates and individual liberty is enjoyed.

Milton supports 'the good old cause' of liberty. In his *Tenure of Kings and Magistrates*, published a fortnight after the execution of Charles I (1649) he emphatically negates the divine right of the rulers. He categorically states, 'the power of the kings and magistrates is nothing else but what is only derivative, transformed, and committed to them in trust from the people to the common good of them all, in whom the power yet remains fundamentally and cannot be taken away from them without a violation of their birth right.' Milton refers to Aristotle and other political writers who have defined a king as one 'who governs to the good and profit of the people and not for his own ends.' He adds 'that to say kings are accountable to none but God, is the overturning of all law and government.' He thinks that it is preposterous to consider kingship as divine. Milton affirms that since 'the king or magistrate holds that authority of the people both originally and naturally for their good in the first place and not for his own, then may the people as oft as they shall judge it for the best, either choose him or reject him, retain him or depose him, though no tyrant, merely by the liberty and right of free born man to be governed as seems to them best.' Milton believes that the people as represented in the parliament have the right to create or alter their form of government. If the ruler violates the laws of justice, the people have the right to punish him.

After the publication of *The Tenure of Kings and Magistrates* Milton is surprised to have an invitation from the Council of State desiring his services in the Foreign Affairs. A month after the publication of *The Tenure*, Milton is appointed Secretary of Foreign Tongues to the Council and he holds that office for eleven years (1649-1660) till the Restoration. The salary is only £290 a year and this is slightly reduced when he becomes blind and needs an assistant to work with him. Milton accepts the offer hoping that he will be of some use to the nation, even though his political opponents choose to call him maliciously 'mercenary Milton.'

Soon after the king's execution a pamphlet, *Eikon Basilike*, supposed to have been written by Charles I himself in his solitude, is published. This immediately becomes popular and forty seven editions of the book appear in Hague and other places in Europe. Even in England the pamphlet produces a wave of sympathy for Charles I. The new government naturally gets shaken and the Council commissions Milton to prepare a fitting rejoinder. Milton prepares *Eikonoklastes* and this is published in October 1649. He defends the Council and justifies its action in beheading the king. In *Eikonoklastes*, Milton 'had an opportunity to defend a rational cultural revolution against the Royalist appeal to the primitive magic of kingship.' (Hill, 170)

A more difficult task awaits Milton for some of the Presbyterians in Scotland get in touch with Salamasius, an eminent Latin scholar and Professor at Leyden, to attack the new government and the English people for regicide. Salamasius happens to be the most reputed scholar in Europe, whereas Milton is almost unknown at that time. Salamasius publishes his vindictive pamphlet in Latin, *Defensio Regio* in November 1649. The Council instructs the Latin Secretary, Milton, to prepare a defence of the English people. The first Defence in Latin is published in 1651. Milton puts himself to a great risk in preparing this pamphlet for even at that time he has lost the use of one eye by accepting the heavy task. But Milton the nationalist disregards the advice of the physician. He says, 'I would not have listened to the voice even of Aesculapius (the god of medicine) himself from the shrine of Epidaurus, in preference to the suggestions of the heavenly monitor within my breath; my resolution was unshaken, though the alternative was either the loss of my sight or the desertion of my duty.'

Milton chooses to lose his vision in performing his sacred duty of justifying 'the good old cause.' This *Defence* brings European fame to Milton and Salamasius the greatest scholar of Europe at that time is discomfited. Salamasius loses his credit in the court of Queen Christiana of Sweden. Milton's nephew Edward comments, 'our little English David had the courage to undertake the great French Goliath.' Milton himself is amused for his sonnet 'To Mr. Cyriack Skinner upon his blindness' speaks of his defence of liberty as his

> noble task
> Of which all Europe rings from side to side.

Milton's command over Latin language makes him vanquish his formidable foe Salamasius. But he has to pay a heavy price, for he becomes totally blind in 1652 at the age of forty four, even though he continues as Latin Secretary till 1660.

Milton's political rivals attribute his blindness to a divine dispensation for traducing the king and defending a bad cause. Milton replies boldly,

> Let them consider . . . that in the solace and the strength which have been infused into me from above, I have been enabled to do the will of God. . . . I would prefer my blindness to yours; yours is a cloud spread over the mind, which darkens both the light of reason and of conscience, mine keeps from my view only the coloured surface of things, while it leaves me at liberty to contemplate the beauty and stability of virtue and of truth.

Milton affirms that his personal loss is for a good cause as he mentions in his sonnet to Skinner in 1655,

> What supports me, dost thou ask?
> The conscience, Friend, to have lost them overplied
> In Liberty's defence, my noble task.

He is able to bear the infirmity because of his firm faith that he is serving 'God's Englishmen.' But he is not allowed to be content with his blindness for another pamphlet in Latin, *Regii Sanguinis Clamor*. (The Royal blood crying to heaven in vengeance on the English parricides) is published attacking Milton and the Council. The editor Alexander More (Morus) is taken by Milton as the real author of the treatise. Even though Morus denies his authorship Milton attacks him ruthlessly. This

Second Defence of the English people written by Milton in Latin, published in 1654 is valuable for the autobiographical passages it contains. Apart from attacking his political opponents, Milton defends himself by referring to his early life, his Italian tour, his poetic, religious and political beliefs. He says that he has never approached anyone for any favour, none knew neither soliciting anything myself or through the medium of my friends, ever beheld me in a supplicating position at the doors of the senate, or the levies of the great.' (*Second Defence*) In the *Second Defence*, Milton also says that 'he alone deserves the appellation of great who either achieves great things himself, or teaches how they may be achieved, or who describes with suitable dignity the great achievements of others.'

Milton's involvement in the cause of liberty even at the expense of losing his eyesight is something supremely sacrificial. But he believes that he has done it for a noble task. Browning in *The Lost Leader* draws the essential difference between Wordsworth and Milton. Wordsworth first supports the cause of liberty, but for 'a handful of silver' forgets all about his idealism. Milton fights for individual liberty and freedom of the nation. Shakespeare is with the people. The *Second Defence* gives a crushing defeat to his foes, but they harp on his blindness as a punishment meted out to him by God for having attacked the divinity of kingship. Milton maintains that he 'only preferred Queen Truth to King Charles.' The two *Defences* of the English people give to Milton a feeling and a satisfaction that 'he had in a way fulfilled his first intention of a poem on the exploits of the English people and statesmen.' (Grierson, 12)

A few weeks before the Restoration Milton publishes a pamphlet *The Ready and Easy Way to Establish a Free Commonwealth* trying to influence Monk and other leaders to have a Republican form of government for England. Milton's concept of a Commonwealth is intended to train citizens who will support the cause of liberty. He cannot understand why a nation 'so valorous and courageous to win their liberty in the field, and when they have won it, should be heartless and unwise in their counsels, as not to know how to use it, value it, what to do with it or with themselves.' (*The Ready and Easy Way*) To him such a state is reprehensible. He firmly believes that a Commonwealth can be like the ancient institutions in Rome, Sparta or Venice.

A free Commonwealth, as Milton imagines, is an institution 'magnanimous, most fearless and confident of its own fair proceedings.' Kingship to him is 'pusillanimous, full of fears, full of jealousies, startled at every umbrage.' Finally in *The Ready and Easy Way* he concludes 'with all hazard I have ventured what I thought my duty to speak in season, and to forewarn the country in time.' He can only cry with the prophet, 'O earth, earth, earth.' He realizes that 'God's Englishmen' have disappointed him.

By the time Milton gives a second edition of *The Ready and Easy Way to Establish a Free Commonwealth* in April 1660, the champion of 'the good old cause' understands that the people are in favour of monarchy. But his unshaken faith in republicanism and contempt for Charles II and his courtiers remains unchanged.

As the author of *The Tenure of Kings*, and *Eikonoklastes*, and as one who has served the Commonwealth as Latin Secretary Milton faces punishment. He was to be hanged the moment monarchy was restored in 1660. His books were burnt, his property was confiscated, he was rendered poor. The sergeant-at-arms took him into custody. Later he was released when the Bill of General Pardon, Indemnity and Oblivion came to his rescue.

Milton considers the nation not yet ripe for a Commonwealth. He wonders why God has withdrawn his protective hand from the nation. He turns to God for an answer. It is in this mood of interrogation that he embarks upon his literary project, 'long choosing and beginning late' of justifying God's ways to men. He thinks that in order 'to turn God's Englishmen to God again, God's ways must be justified to them.' 'The good old cause' tentatively seems to have failed, despite his sincere service to the nation and his personal suffering. Yet peculiarly his own republican views become the source of inspiration for the Whig party that comes into shape in 1688. Especially after 1688, his political views get acceptance and recognition from the radical Whigs.

Milton in the evening of his life acquires a spiritual enlightenment that God's ways are essentially just and that surrender to God's will is the noblest form of human existence. Instead of writing a national epic with a limited appeal, the blind poet like the blind prophets of the world, sings of the destiny of mankind and its relationship with God. Milton wants to be a national poet, but God's grace makes him one of the immortal bards of the world.

The Grand Whig

Immediately after the Restoration in 1660 Milton goes back to his original literary project of writing an epic, a tragedy and a brief epic. From 1660-1674, in the last fourteen years of his life, Milton no longer actively participates in the Revolutionary programme he has followed as Secretary for Foreign Tongues in the Commonwealth. His view of the English people as 'a noble and puissant nation rousing herself like a strong man after sleep, and shaking her invincible locks' (*Areopagitica*), was rudely shaken.

In the years of his Latin Secretaryship he imagined that England was providentially led to reformation. After the Restoration he felt that 'God's Englishmen' had given him a shocking experience. The same nation that had fought for individual liberty and freedom of the country had tamely accepted the 'Egyptian bondage,' the restoration of monarchy. His immense faith in the glory of the nation had resulted in his loss of vision and his narrow escape from being hanged. He was no doubt pardoned but he had to lose his savings of £2000 as a consequence of the Restoration. His house in Bread Street was burnt in the Great Fire of 1666. He was humiliated and abused by his political opponents. But undoubtedly he was 'one of the first Englishmen publicly to defend the right of the people to call their kings to account, just as in 1660 he was the last Englishman to nail his colours to the republican mast.' (Hill, 167)

Even in those last fourteen years of his life, 1660-1674, Milton's disciples and admirers, styling themselves as Nonconformists, followed Milton's prose tracts, and spoke his language in the political conflicts of the age. His name was well established in Europe through his works in Latin and English. His revolutionary programme influenced several Englishmen denouncing the Cavilier-Church orthodoxy. *The Nonconformists* mostly followed Milton's prose pamphlets, *The Tenure of Kings and Magistrates, Eikonoklastes* and the two *Defences of the English People*.

Especially in *Eikonoklastes*, Milton had an opportunity to defend a national, cultural revolution. Some of the followers of Milton like Hunt and Johnson adapted Milton's writings to suit the needs of the age. Needham, Cyriack Skinner, Nathan Paget, Hack and several Fellows of the Royal Society like Henry Oldenburg, Abraham Hill, John Audrey, John Winthrop, Jr, became Milton's associates and admirers in those years when he was away from the political arena. Those were also the years when he was often in solitude 'with dangers compast round' and with the sons of Belial, the courtiers of Charles II, shouting at him and ridiculing him especially very late in the night.

The Cavilier-Church opposition considered Milton, an antagonist not to be reckoned with lightly. Thomas Flatman ironically referred to Milton as 'that grand Whig.' The Cavilier party in power realized that it had to counter Milton's influence with a campaign of vilification and falsehood. By Tory admission Milton was 'an oracle and the classic of the opposition, almost dangerous antagonist, a great Whig.' (Sensabaugh, 125) Milton was feared for his rhetoric and for his intellectual eminence. He was viewed 'as an oracle of political wisdom,' 'a great noble genius.' Milton was accorded even by his political opponents 'a position commensurate with that which Cromwell secured on the field of battle or Henry Vane in the House of Commons.' (*Ibid.*, 2) Milton was recognised as one who had played a leading role in shaping opinion during the Puritan Revolution. In fact Milton proved himself to be a mighty champion of intellectual and political freedom.

But the most insinuating attack on Milton by the Cavilier-Church opposition was that he was a Jesuit in disguise. The story that 'Milton was a Jesuit in disguise' seemed indeed so credible that Edward Petit developed it further in *The Vision of Purgatory*, a satire on political events attending the debates over the succession. (*Ibid.*, 118) Milton was supposed to be frequently visiting a Popish club and Hancock saw the analogy between Milton and the Pope for both seemed to favour anti-monarchical doctrines. Thomas Long argued how delighted Milton was in supporting Pope. This was one type of criticism that the opposition levelled against Milton, mostly to slur his reputation.

Even after his death Milton's influence on the Nonconformists of his day remained to be great though they might not have, as yet, openly owned him as their leader. But his opponents, the Cavilier-Church opposition, attacked Milton even from a personal angle as a 'blind Beetle' and 'Mercenary Milton.' His opponents sincerely believed that God had punished him for his excesses in attacking the divinity of kingship, and they thought that Milton had accepted the Secretaryship in the Commonwealth for money. These two charges and several others were levelled against Milton. Some Cavilier-Church opposition to Milton appeared without vituperation, some showed derision, some purposely vilified his character, but all of them feared the influence of Milton on the Nonconformists who fought for the liberty of conscience. Milton, even in the last years of his life, remained a source of strength to the Nonconformists and other groups associated with them.

Especially after the publication of his monumental epic *Paradise Lost* in 1667, the nation, to a large extent, accepts him as a distinguished poet who has brought glory to the country. Denham, the parliamentarian comes into 'the house [the parliament] with a sheet wet from the press in his hands' and proudly declares, 'Part of the Noblest poem that ever was written in any language or in any Age.' (Wolf, Section 117) This was the accolade generally paid to Milton after the publication of the epic even by his political opponents. In fact Milton's political followers were larger than the admiring readers of *Paradise Lost* at that time. His contribution to the Commonwealth decisions and discussions was equally great. Ambassadors from foreign countries used to meet the Latin Secretary, Milton, with respect and admiration. In a well-known passage Aubrey tells us that 'Cromwell and Milton were the main sights which foreigners wished to see in England.' (Hill, 227) Even after 1660 these visits continued. While referring to the Oldenburg Safeguard, Mylius the diplomat from the Count of Oldenburg in Germany observes that the Parliamentary Commission of the Commonwealth is seated, whereas Milton remains standing. Mylius prophetically states that 'those seated men of power are transitory, whose presence that day will be remembered only because their mere secretary standing beside them is in fact *the great* Milton.' (Miller, 70)

Milton's supreme influence on the Whigs is felt when they openly recognise him as their leader and spokesman in the Glorious Revolution of 1688. The Cavilier-Church opposition and the Nonconformists from 1688 onwards function as Tories and Whigs respectively. It looks as though Milton has arisen from his grave as a great exemplar to speak to his disciples and inspire them with his revolutionary ideas. When the Tories also get disappointed with the aggressive Catholic policies of James II, most of them become friendly with the Whigs and they call themselves Williamites. Milton's leading prose tracts like *The Tenure of Kings, Eikonoklastes* still inspire the Whigs. Milton definitely 'contributed to the growing Whig power in leading the voice of support of the Williamites' cause.' (Sensabaugh, 127)

The Tenure of Kings and Magistrates appears in 1689 as an adaptation to suit the needs of the Revolutionary Settlement of 1688. A reprint of *Eikonoclastes* is given with the 'Anglesey Memorandum' in 1690 to argue against the Jacobite cause. The Memorandum reveals the true author of the *Eikon Basilike* as Bishop Gauden, not Charles I, and it exposes the tyrannies of Charles I. Charles Blout gives an adaptation of *Areopagitica* in 1693. The Glorious Revolution of 1688 bringing William and Mary to the throne restores Milton to his days of Commonwealth. The enthusiasm of the Whigs in the eighteenth century makes them openly express their indebtedness to Milton's political views, even though his opponents have recognised him even a decade earlier as the Grand

Whig. Milton attains a position for which he has struggled to achieve in the Puritan Revolution. His two nephews Edward and John pay eloquent tributes to his memory as the Whigs become triumphant. Milton is enshrined in the hearts of the Whigs as a great leader of liberty.

The eighteenth century opens with Milton 'firmly established as a great spokesman of the Whig party and a great defender of the rights and liberties of the English people (Sensabaugh, 180). No other writer has ever received such a recognised place of leadership in the political affairs of the country as Milton did. The Whigs acknowledge that singular achievement of Milton wholeheartedly. Apart from Milton's nephews, other literary writers of the day celebrate Milton's glory as a poet and a political writer.

But the greatest champion of Milton is John Toland. He published *The Works of John Milton* in 1697, and in the next year he gave a complete edition of Milton's prose, both in Latin and English. In 1699 he published *Amyntor*, the life of Milton. Toland takes Milton as a good man of political wisdom. Several other scholars also pay accolades to Milton as a compendium of virtue. His prose pamphlets get reprinted. The Jacobites still campaign to discredit Milton, but Toland and other disciples maintain that Milton's contribution to the strength of the Whig party is immense. Reasonably it can be stated that to the 'triumph of the main European tradition modified by Puritan and Whig thought, Milton made a notable contribution through the revolution, through his revolutionary program for man and society.' (Sensabaugh, 204)

Toland's first collection of poetry in 1697 and his

defence of Milton's life in *Amyntor* establish Milton as a great defender of the liberty of the English people. The Whigs raise him to great heights of political wisdom and literary fame. No doubt Milton had generously supported his country with the aid of his pen. Among early Whigs he was one of the greatest.

However Milton's letter to Peter Heimbach in 1666 is quoted by some critics to show that he could not have been quite happy in the last years of his life. Milton states in the letter, 'One of those Virtues, however has not requited me handsomely for my hospitality. For the virtue you call statesmanship (which I would rather have you call loyalty to my country) after captivating me with her fair sounding name, has so to speak, almost left me without a country.' (Tillyard) This may have been a passing mood of disillusionment of Milton in the first few years of the Restoration. Based on such utterances, there is a tendency among the critics to associate Milton's last years as one of contempt for the mob for he presents them as 'herd confused' through the Son of God in *Paradise Regained.* The Son of God caustically comments dismissing glory and people's praise when Satan refers to them in *Paradise Regained*, Bk III. The Son says, 'And what the people but a herd confused/ A miscellaneous rabble.' (ll. 49-50) The suggestion is that one cannot put too much faith in popular applause. But this is only a dramatic speech, not necessarily Milton's view. Milton does not seem to be cynical or frustrated in the last years of his life. Fallen on 'evil days' and 'evil tongues,' with faith in God and with the realization that God's ways are essentially just, though we often doubt 'what the unsearchable dispose/Of Highest Wisdom brings about,' Milton surrenders himself to

God and the muse of poetry. He does not seem to be unduly cynical or self-defensive, instead, he 'summons God to judgment and finally pronounces him not guilty.' (Hill, 463) Far from the madding crowd, Milton the grand Whig survives not only as an eminent poet but also as a great political leader of the nation. One is inclined to think that Milton will endure 'while Oratory, Politics or History bear any esteem among men.' (Sensabaugh, VIII: 168)

Milton Agonistes

The word 'Agonistes' is used in the sense of a champion, though it may also mean a wrestler, a struggler. Milton takes on himself the stupendous task of justifying God's ways to men. Restoration of monarchy in 1660 puts a tremendous strain on Milton's acceptance of God's justice for 'in the forties he had confidently believed that he was serving a God who specially favoured England, who was about to use the English people to perform great deeds on his behalf.' (Hill, 244) The collapse of the Revolution makes Milton question the ways of God. He has to justify to himself the reasonableness of God's actions before he can convince others about God's justice.'

In the last years of his life Milton acquires a spiritual enlightenment whereby he realizes that God's ways are essentially just, though they may appear to be mysterious and inscrutable. He communicates this rich, religious experience through his three long poems, *Paradise Lost*, *Samson Agonistes* and *Paradise Regained*. In his major epic *Paradise Lost* he tries to bring heavenly matter to earthly level. It is generally felt that when Milton chooses to 'assert Eternal Providence/And justify the ways of God to men' he is embarking on the ambitious design of describing 'what cannot be described, the agency of spirits.' (Johnson, 67) It is also true that 'though Milton was describing the indescribable he was not describing the undescribed.' (R.M. Frye, 3) Milton follows the doctrine or accommodation whereby the representation of God in Scripture has to be 'accommodated to man's understanding by being reduced to language in which human intelligence can comprehend.' (Leland, 7) The theory of accommodation was not limited to theologians but was accepted and voiced by poets and men of letters in that age. Especially the Protestant writers of the age had no hesitation in using the doctrine of accommodation.

Milton follows the technique of presenting God as one of the speaking characters in the epic. In the Indian epics too, the *Ramayana* and the *Mahabharata* Rama and Krishna figure as mortals even though the godlike form in them is also retained. So in the descriptive accounts Milton bestows on God the conventional epithets of godhead. In Book III of *Paradise Lost* the angels sing of God as

> Omnipotent
> Immutable, Immortal, Infinite,
> Eternal King, the Author of all being.

Milton's God has all the divine attributes and 'the traditional exposition of God's attributes furnishes one of the most enduring aspects of the affirmative approach.' (Patrides 10) In Book V Adam and Eve pray to God referring to his magnificence, his superb creation and his almightiness. God is the one Supreme Being and he is the 'Eternal Father.' So an anthropomorphic manifestation of God becomes inevitable in any literary work of art where God happens to be a speaking character. The theological tradition 'of knowing God through analogy to human experience appears in the most specific form . . . in the doctrine of accommodation.' (Leland, 141)

Milton in Book III presents God mostly in the human form arguing logically and explaining his ways in the most reasonable form. God poses the question.

> so will fall
> He and his faithless progeny; whose fault?
> Whose but his own?

God with his foreknowledge can visualize a situation where Man may go wrong and merit his fall. Milton explains Man's relationship with God in Book III in a clear, logical fashion. Man is given free will, the will to serve God or the devil. So Adam and Eve are the 'authors to themselves in all/Both what they judge and what they choose.' They are free to decide for themselves the right path or the wrong one. God observes,

> I formed them free, and free they must remain,
> Till they enthrall themselves.

If they choose to fall, no one can help them. They are not predestined to fall, there is a likelihood of Man being deceived. However God assures the angels in Heaven. 'Man . . . shall find grace.' God excels in 'Mercy and Justice' but 'Mercy first and last shall brightest shine.' Even though God has to do justice by punishing the wrong ones,' Man shall find grace.

Milton exercises all the imaginable arguments to show the reasonableness of God's actions. When God says,

Man shall not quite be lost, but saved who will,
Yet not of will in him, but grace in me
Freely vouchsafed,

we hear the voice of God as God who is all mercy to the erring Man. God also promises that

To prayer, repentance, and obedience due,
Though but endeavoured with sincere intent,
Mine ear shall not be lost; mine eye not shut.

God adds that Man shall be saved provided

Some other able and as willing, pay
The rigid satisfaction, death for death.

This condition of death for death sounds more earthly than heavenly, but it is a test of obedience. Only the Son of God accepts the challenging task of redeeming the sin of the first Man. God finally sums up that 'heavenly love shall outdo hellish hate.'

Even though Milton's God opens the talk like a clever logician, he ends up as a benevolent God prepared to sacrifice his Son for the sake of Man. In *Paradise Lost* divine omnipotence is implied rather than affirmed. The Son of God functions as the Mediator, the Interceptor, the 'unexampled love/Love nowhere to be found less than divine.'

Milton introduces two episodes in *Paradise Lost*, the first one consists of Books V, VI, VII and VIII and the last one is given to Books XI and XII. In the first episode, God sends Raphael to inform Adam of the coming events and advise him to love only

What higher in her [Eve's] society thou findest
Attractive, human, rational

and not be a slave to his passion. Raphael realizes that Adam is overcome with feminine charm and that over-fondness for Eve may lead to his fall. Adam warmly describes in Book VIII his association with Eve and confesses that

All higher knowledge in her presence falls
Degraded. Wisdom or discourse with her
Loses discountenanced, and like Folly shows;
Authority and Reason on her wait,
As one intended first, not after made
Occasionally, and to consummate all
Greatness of mind and nobleness their seat
Build in her loveliest, and create an awe
About her, as a guard angelic placed.

Adam confesses his infatuation for Eve. His inordinate liking for her and his absolute faith in her supreme position indicate his weakness and suggest his fall. If Adam chooses to fall by making his primary obligation to God secondary, and his secondary obligation to Eve primary, one can reasonably expect the topsyturvydom in Adam's relationship with God. So Raphael warns Adam,

stand fast or fall
Free in thine own arbitrement it lies,
Perfect within, no outward aid requires;
And all temptation to transgress repel.

The insistence here, as in God's speech in Book III, is on free will. Adam is free to stand or fall. He is perfection itself, he needs no external aid. He can resist the temptation if he wills it.

Despite all this advice Adam goes wrong mostly because of a human weakness in him. Even though he disobeys God he still gets our sympathetic reaction as he is human in his affection for Eve. When Eve eats the forbidden fruit, instead of finding fault with her, he feels the bond of nature drawing him to her for he says,

> What thou art is mine,
> Our state cannot be severed, we are one,
> One flesh, to lose thee were to lose myself.

His resolution is to die with her. Even if God creates another Eve she will not be dear to him. He tells Eve,

> Flesh of flesh,
> Bone of my bone thou art and from thy state
> Mine never be parted, bliss or woe. (Book IX)

Together they live, together they die. This togetherness appeals to the reader, though he realizes that Adam is committing sin. Milton's artistic creation renders Adam and Eve, Everyman and Everywoman to be sympathized with and not to be condemned.

The last two books, Books XI and XII comprising the second episode, are often considered to be an unnecessary intrusion into the epic structure. They are supposed to be inartistic (Lewis, 175) and pessimistic (Rajan, 83). Book X still leaves the reader unreconciled to God's ways. Milton has to show the epic purification of Man and Woman whereby they understand the justice involved in God's ways. In these two books after seeing the visions and hearing the narrative given by Michael

Adam is recreated and regenerated. When Adam and Eve tend to question God's ways and find fault with each other in Book X, God takes pity on them and sends Michael instructing him to drive out the sinful pair, 'though sorrowing, yet in peace.' Michael exhorts Adam through visions in Book XI giving an account of Adam's posterity over two thousand years with the huge flood and Noah's ark working for a second world of regenerated humanity.

In Book XII Michael narrates the future events, ultimately bringing the historical account to the birth of the Saviour. Milton with all the zeal for the Messiah describes,

> Yet at his birth a star
> Unseen before in Heaven proclaims him come,
> And guides the Eastern sages, who inquire
> His place to offer incense, myrh and gold.

Milton recapitulates the descriptive account of his earlier poem, *The Nativity Ode*. In these last two books Milton presents the apocalyptic stage of complete goodness, perfection and innocence through a process of elevating human nature from degeneration to regeneration.

When Michael tells Adam that the Son of God will endure Adam's punishment 'by coming in the flesh/To a reproachful life and cursed death' Adam exclaims,

> O goodness infinite, goodness immense,
> That all this good of evil shall produce
> And evil to turn to good! more wonderful
> Than that by which creation first brought forth
> Light out of darkness!

expressing his unbounded joy in understanding the intricate ways of God. Adam wonders whether he should repent of his sin

> or rejoice
> Much more, that much more good
> thereof shall spring,
> To God more glory, more good to men.

Adam understands the benevolence of God in sending his Son to atone for his sin. While seeming to be harsh on him, God is definitely kind to him. Milton succeeds in showing the reasonableness of God's actions. What Adam has lost, the Son of God will regain by vanquishing Satan, Sin and Death. Milton also refers to the millennium when the Son and the Saints will rule the world with love and justice to mankind. There will be

> New Heavens, new Earth, Ages of endless date,
> Founded in righteousness and peace and love,
> To bring forth fruits, Joy and eternal Bliss.

Milton hopefully, optimistically envisages a golden age of golden deeds conferring joy and bliss on the world. Righteousness, justice, peace and love will prevail in this world. Adam becomes reconciled with God's ways. He realizes that the true Paradise is to be found within. Milton transmutes the popular myth in retelling that 'Paradise within is won only after the external visible Paradise has been lost.' (Will, 379) Eve too is recreated through dreams and Adam and Eve leave Paradise recognising that God will be with them wherever they go. Hand in hand, Adam and Eve take 'their solitary way.' It is precisely 'this joining of hands which is so extremely rare in art.' (R.M Frye, 282) We are aware of the human aspect of their solitariness, but we have the comforting thought of the presence of God with them in this world of wilderness.

Milton successfully manages the difficult task of interpreting matter beyond human comprehension, of likening spiritual matter to corporeal form. It is indeed a challenging problem for Milton to make unapparent things apparent, incredible deeds credible. This he achieves by introducing the doctrine of accommodation, apocalyptic visions and images based on classical myths and scriptural matter. On the whole he succeeds in familiarizing the unfamiliar, the justice in God's ways. The last two books give to the epic a solemnity and transcendence. Especially 'when we consider what Adam and Eve have lost and what now lies before them, Milton's achievement seems to be little short of the miraculous.' (R.M. Frye, 314)

Milton is like Abdiel, the faithful among the faithless, justifying the ways of God to men. The three great poems reveal three phases of God's ways to men, the mercy meted out to Man in *Paradise Lost*, the inexplicable manner in which God comes to the rescue of his faithful in *Samson Agonistes*, the unbounded love of God in sending the Son to redeem the sin of Man in *Paradise Regained*. In all these three poems, the intriguing, amazing aspect of divine dispensation figures. Milton is keen on exposing the justice in God's ways and the reasonableness of his actions. In this respect Milton's own religious experience is transmuted and transformed into something universal. This is done by Milton consistently through a process of interpreting the scriptural and biblical material through coherent argumentation. Whereas his brief epic *Paradise Regained* is the culmination of his effort to translate his religious experience into something understandable, in the other two poems *Paradise Lost* and *Samson Agonistes* Milton mostly depends on the technique of interrogation of and reconciliation with God's ways.

Especially the Old Testament story of Samson appeals to him as a convenient medium for projecting his own rich, religious experience in a universal form. Milton finds it easier to argue and confirm his belief in God's justice in *Samson Agonistes*. The play opens with Samson in prison violently questioning God's ways. At his birth angels twice foretold that he would become the deliverer of Israel. With biting sarcasm he says,

> Ask for this great Deliverer now, and find him
> Eyeless in Gaza at the mill with slaves;
> Himself in bonds under Philistian yoke;

Also he suffers from blindness. He bemoans,

> O loss of sight of thee I most complain!
> Blind among enemies, O worse than chains,

It is a life half dead, 'a living death.'

The Chorus sees Samson as 'one past hope, abandoned.' The questions posed by Samson arraigning God's justice in his moments of gloom and despair are generally raised by others in similar circumstances. So Milton takes up the fundamental question of the justice involved in God's ways. The Chorus sees Samson 'abandoned' in a deplorable mental state. The Chorus feels that Samson serves as a typical example of

> how much from the top of wondrous glory,
> Strongest of mortal men,
> To lowest pitch of abject fortune fall.

The Chorus however tries to console Samson by suggesting that

> Just are the ways of God,
> And justifiable to Men
> Unless there be who think not God at all.

Samson's father Manoa finds fault with God's dispensation in having allowed 'The miracle of men' his son, to be 'ensnared, assaulted, led bound' to work with slaves. He thinks that at least for the sake of former glorious deeds Samson should not have been subjected to such 'foul indignities.'

Later the Chorus examines God's ways in a critical manner and considers them unpredictable. Especially those 'solemnly elected' suffer most at the hands of God. When they are at the height of their glory God seems to change his countenance and withdraw his supporting hand irrespective of the service they have done to him. The Chorus comments that his heroes elevated to high positions are unceremoniously dropped by God leaving them to their fate. In this lengthy passage (ll. 2667-2704) the Chorus is unsparingly critical of God's attitude towards his own heroes. Oblique references are supposed to have been made to the indignities heaped on the remains of Cromwell, Ireton and Bradshaw being desecrated after the Restoration. Unjust tribunals may refer to Henry Vane, condemned and executed in 1662. References to sickness, disease and poverty may be to the poet himself. Finally the Chorus concludes,

> Just or unjust, alike seem miserable,
> For oft alike, both come to evil end.

God does not seem to differentiate between the deserved and the undeserved persons, all come to be punished by him most indiscriminately. The Chorus reproduces the typical human feelings in misery when the whole blame is put on God's ways. Milton is at his best in giving a detailed picture of the human evaluation of misery in terms of unseen fate or cruel God.

Just when the Chorus finishes its tirade against God, Dalila comes to tempt Samson to go back to her. The process of self-revelation has started in Samson. He realizes that pride in him has brought him to that stage. In those days of intoxicating power and sensual delights Samson moves 'like a petty God.' He confesses,

> I walked about admired of all and dreaded
> On hostile ground none daring any affront,
> Then swollen with pride into the snare I fell
> Of fair fallacious looks, venereal trains.

Milton introduces the homiletic tradition of sin, repentance and expiation. Samson is now brought to the level of penitence and he is to be tempted and tested before he can be accepted by God. The play is viewed as Hellenic, Hebraic and Christian. Hanford thinks that *Samson Agonistes* is 'Hellenic tragedy restored' for a seventeenth century audience. It is even suggested that Samson-Apocalypse link may hint at some 'political dimensions.' Some have seen the play as 'a near-allegory of the Puritan cause in the Post-Restoration England, while others have seen Samson as a figure of Puritan hopes in the revolution.' (Lewalaski, 1970: 1061) The play mostly reflects Miltonic thought content with a Christian background. Samson has to face fiery tests. Milton's confirmed view, as expressed in *Comus*, is that God purposely puts man in the midst of plenty so that he may be tempted and tested.

Dalila comes bedecked 'like a fair flower surcharged with dew.' Already Samson condemns himself for having revealed God's secret to her and even the 'Gentiles in their parables condemn' such persons 'To their abyss and horrid pains confined.' In that mood of total revulsion for his deed, Samson finds Dalila a cunning sorceress. He condemns her ruthlessly. Dalila tries to defend herself by suggesting that what she has done is for public good. But Samson remains unyielding to her importunities of love. Dalila's visit makes him mentally alert. He is roused from his state of lethargy and despair. Samson tells the Chorus that God has sent her to debase him and aggravate his folly. The Chorus praises Samson for having resisted the temptation for 'virtue which breaks through all opposition/ And all temptation can remove,/ Most shines and most is accepted above.' These lines remind us of *Comus* where temptation resisted by the Lady becomes virtue of great esteem.

Samson is exposed to another trial. Harapha comes to him in a boastful manner, to see Samson of legendary fame. If he has been there on those occasions where Samson's valour was praised, he would have definitely vanquished him. Harapha provokes Samson with such insulting, insinuating talk. Samson's physical strength, revived through the growth of the hair on his head, gives him the courage to challenge Harapha to a single combat. Samson says that it can easily be seen whose God is stronger, his or Harapha's through a combat. If he chooses, Harapha can be seconded by his God. Harapha's visit is likened to the visit of James, Prince of Wales, to see Milton the rebel. Like Harapha James too goes back protesting against the blind poet's audacity and daringness in reviling kingship. Harapha leaves Samson 'somewhat crestfallen/ Stalking with unconscionable strides.' But the Chorus anticipates some trouble for Samson.

Samson is commissioned to participate in the festival of Dagon. He refuses to attend for he cannot abuse 'the consecrated gift/ Of strength, again returning' with his hair. But soon revelation comes to him. He feels 'some rousing motions' in him and his thoughts tend towards something extraordinary. He asserts prophetically,

> This day will be remarkable in my life
> By some great act, or of my days the last.

Samson having resisted the temptations becomes God's chosen servant again. He is reclaimed by God. He chooses to participate in the festival of Dagon, and it looks as though the Philistines have signed their death warrant in ordering him to be present at the festival. Intoxicated by wine, the revellers wish to disgrace Samson, but the true God gives to Samson a lofty death 'at once both to destroy and be destroyed.' Samson pulls down the edifice on the heads of the Philistines and on his own head. Through death Samson is ennobled. Manoa and the Chorus still dream of eyesight being restored to Samson for they think that restoration of eyesight is absolutely necessary for making Samson the deliverer. They fail to realize that where God's grace is extended blindness is no obstacle at all in achieving life's objective.

Samson throughout the play is 'the greatly suffering and struggling hero, engaged, as are all the Elect, in the conquest of himself, in the process of spiritual growth.' (Lewalaski, 1970: 1054) It is also felt that Samson succeeds only when he accepts humiliation for he fails 'as the Athlete of God' and succeeds as 'the Fool of God.' (Stein, 66) Through his fall he learns the great lesson of willing submission and unswerving loyalty to God.

Samson Agonistes is viewed as 'the tragedy of the Apocalypse for Samson becomes the instrument of God's power and he has to fulfil God's mission. *Samson Agonistes* is also examined typologically whereby Samson's suffering is seen as a type of Christ's passion and the destruction of the Philistines through his martyrdom 'as type of Christ's defeat of Satan, Sin and death at his crucifixion.' (Lewalaski, 1970: 1054) Samson is seen as a Christ figure.

Samson Agonistes embodies the religious experience of Milton. Unlike a typical tragedy, Samson ends on a lofty note of idealism and reaffirmation of faith in God's ways and God's justice. Milton through the Chorus expresses his felt experience,

> All is best, though we oft doubt
> What the unsearchable dispose
> Of Highest Wisdom brings about,
> And ever best found in the close.

God's inscrutable, mysterious ways may be puzzling, for unexpectedly he returns and enables his devoted worshippers to fulfil their God-given tasks. Milton triumphantly illustrates through Samson that those who love God are truly rewarded. The play ends on a note of peace and consolation with 'calm of mind, all passion spent.' The philosophic calm expresses the felt religious experience of Milton and also of the playgoers.

Though *Samson Agonistes* has a religious and theological background intended mostly for justifying God's ways to men, it has all the ingredients of a tragedy, specially a Greek tragedy. Samson falls from the heights of glory, but unlike a tragic hero he is recreated and regenerated. Peculiarly enough in *Samson Agonistes* 'the tragedy ends in triumph and the carnival in catastrophe.' (Frye, 108) Samson is both a sinner and a martyr. Finally he becomes the deliverer and achieves victory over his foes. But 'suffering though it may be a means of grace, is suffering still, and death though it be the price of such a victory, and though it even comes as a release from suffering, is still death.' (Woodhouse, 111) Milton succeeds in showing God's ways as essentially just, at the same time he produces a tragedy glorifying martyrdom.

Unlike in the two poems, *Paradise Lost* and *Samson Agonistes* where Milton chooses to expose God's ways to a critical examination, in *Paradise Regained* he presents the Son of God as the exalted man, the perfect man who regains Paradise lost by the first Man. From this angle the thematic content is a continuation of the earlier epic where Milton states that the greater Man will restore and regain the blissful seat, Paradise. In the opening lines of *Paradise Regained* Milton refers to the theme,

> I, who erewhile the happy garden sung
> By one man's disobedience lost, now sing
> Recovered Paradise to all mankind,
> By one man's firm obedience fully tried
> Through all temptation, and the tempter foiled

In all his wiles, defeated and repulsed,
And Eden raised in the waste wilderness.

As in *Comus*, in the brief epic, temptation figures as a means of exposing the Son of God to a severe testing of his heroic virtue. Milton firmly believes that 'a good temptation is that whereby God tempts even the righteous for the purpose of proving them, not as though he were ignorant of the disposition of their hearts, but for the purpose of exercising or manifesting their faith or patience as in the case of Abraham and Job or of lessening their self-confidence and reproving their confidence.' (*Christian Doctrine)*

So the heroic virtue as contemplated in *Paradise Regained* refers to moral values, ethical idealism and establishment of righteousness in the world. Milton has patient Job in mind when he portrays the Son of God, patiently accepting all the temptations posed by Satan. The perfect man, by merit called the Son of God, has to conquer Sin and Death and overcome Satanic wiles. He has to enter the 'great duel, not of arms/But to vanquish by wisdom hellish wiles.' The Son of God even from his early childhood understands his mission of doing 'public good' and promoting 'all truth/All righteous things.' He has to bring redemption to mankind.

Paradise Regained is essentially a philosophic poem where the exalted man resists all temptations with faith in himself and faith in God. In the first conflict Satan appears as an aged man. He wants the Son of God to convert stones into bread so that the whole humanity can be relieved of hunger. The Son of God immediately replies that man does not live by bread only. He recognizes the Arch-fiend who confesses that he is 'that spirit unfortunate/Who leagued with millions more in rash revolt' and is driven out to the bottomless deep. This humility is apparently another guise whereby Satan wants to overpower the Son of God.

The banquet-wealth-glory sequence is a greater ordeal for the Son of God. Satan places before the Son a rich banquet with all the delicacies of the world culled together, tempting to the eye. Milton seems to recapture the world of romances, of Ariosto and Spenser, of gorgeous feasts in describing the banquet for the Son of God. Satan tells him that they are not fruits forbidden and no interdict is laid on the food, slyly referring to the interdict imposed on Adam. The Son refuses to accept the pompous delicacies for he counts the specious gifts as guiles.

In the next phase of temptation the Son of God is offered wealth as 'a source of honour, friends, conquests and realms.' But the Son refers to David, Gideon and Jeptha who have achieved great renown though born poor. The Son holds the view that

> he, who reigns within himself and rules
> Passions, desires and fears, is more a king,
> Which every wise and virtuous man attains.

He also thinks that knowing God and serving Him is more kingly than to be a ruler. In all these replies Christ appears to recognise as types of himself and of his moral teaching the noblest ethical ideals of antiquity—the Aristotelian magnanimous man, the Stoic man, the Platonic-Socratic just man or philosopher.

Satan then tries to tempt the Son with the need for attaining glory and receiving popular applause by referring to Alexander, Africanus, Pompey and others. The perfect man dismisses the whole concept of public acclaim and personal glory. He sees the glory as 'the blaze of men' and the people as 'a herd confused,' 'A miscellaneous rabble, who extol/Things vulgar.' This sweeping condemnation of public applause is considered by some critics as a personal view of the poet based on his aristocratic exclusiveness. But this is only a dramatic speech suited for the occasion. Perfect men all over the world work for the good of others, not for their personal gain. In the Indian context such men tend to detach themselves from worldly riches and entanglements. A 'Jnani' possessing wisdom does not involve himself in material gains. The Son of God is a 'Jnani' who has to work for the betterment of mankind through his example. In this banquet-wealth-glory temptation Christ identifies himself with Job.

Satan then suggests that the Son should have a kingdom as he is supposed to free Israel from the Roman yoke. The Saviour politely replies that 'all things are best fulfilled in their time/And time there is for all things.' He also hints that his rise will mean Satan's fall. He says,

> Knowest thou not that my rising is thy fall,
> And my promotion will be thy destruction.

Satan replies almost imitating the Son, 'let that come when it comes.' Then Satan has a quixotic idea of asking the Son to subordinate himself to him for offering the Saviour all the kingdoms of the world. Satan wants to provoke the Son by suggesting such a condition. But the Son is unmoved.

Satan is not abashed. He suggests that the Saviour should become famous through learning and by acquiring the knowledge of the Gentiles for 'all knowledge is not vouched in Moses' law.' He should also refute the 'idolisms, traditions, paradoxes of the Gentiles.' He wants him to think of Socrates as a model. The Saviour calmly replies,

> he who receives
> Light from above, from the fountain of light,
> No other doctrine needs, though granted true.

Here again the Son flouts the worldly values, learning and scholarship.

Condemnation of scholarship by a reputed scholar of European fame like Milton has come in for a good deal of criticism. But 'Christ's vehement rejection of knowledge offered in place of Wisdom is firmly grounded in the tradition which identified God as the substance and source of wisdom.' (Lewalaski, 1966: 298) According to Indian thought content a 'Jnani' acquires 'Jnana' wisdom, through an awareness of his responsibility to God. Christ is a 'Jnani.'

Satan raises a storm of hideousness and ghastliness to perplex the Son. But the Son with his Jobean wisdom remains unshaken. The tower temptation is the final onslaught on the Son. Satan like a 'hippogrif' bears the Son through the sublime air and in a challenging tone asks the Son to stand on the highest pinnacle of the temple in Jerusalem. He tells the Son,

> There stand, if thou wilt stand; to stand upright
> Will ask thee skill; I to thy Father's house
> Have brought thee, and highest placed, highest is best;

> Now show the progeny; if not to stand
> Cast thyself down safely, if Son of God;

With biting sarcasm Satan tells the Son that he is safe in the highest place. The Son warns Satan, 'Tempt not the Lord thy God' and stands safely on the pinnacle. Satan falls, he is vanquished. The tower temptation is the climax to the great combat of good and evil. In the conventional sense it is 'a violent and hellish temptation' and it is seen as 'a means . . . of shaking Christ's faith with terror and fear what might become of him, being now delivered into the hands of Satan.' (Taylor, 190) The tower episode 'is at one level an attempted murder of Christ.' (Lewalaski, 1966: 306) The duel is fought and by vanquishing Satan the Son

> hast regained lost Paradise,
> And frustrated the conquest fraudulent.

Paradise Regained is a brief epic with a Christian background. The Son of God is the grand hero of the epic and his heroic virtue lies in 'the well of mankind' and in resisting temptations with patience and wisdom. The brief epic is 'traditionally a poem of heroic action' and 'Christ has not only overcome temptation, but as the word of God, he has solved the verbal riddle of human life, putting all the words which are properly attributes of God into their faithful context.' (Hughes) Milton's sublime hero, the Son of God, is 'the true wayfaring Christian.'

All the three poems end on a note of lofty idealism glorifying God's ways, and the three heroes are public men blessed by God, not private individuals. Milton Agonistes proves himself to be the champion of God in showing that God's ways are justifiable to men. The three long poems amply demonstrate the reasonableness of God's actions. As Milton affirms in *Samson Agonistes*, we are inclined to think that 'All is best,' though we may often doubt what God gives us. We realize God's benevolence and grace only in the close as it has happened to Samson in the final stage. Especially the lofty endings to these three long poems clearly illustrate God's grace extended to mankind in a mysterious but just manner. The poems of righteousness and justice restore 'calm of mind, all passion lost.'

Hail, Native Language

Milton's apostrophe, 'Hail, native language' finds its unique place in the poem *At a Vacation Exercise*, written in his nineteenth year, while he was a student in Cambridge university. The poem opens with these lines,

> Hail, native language, that by sinews weak
> Didst move my first endeavouring tongue to speak,

expressing Milton's firm faith in his native language not yet developed in all its glory. Scholarship at that time was understood as proficiency in classical languages and Greek and Latin were taught even in high schools. English did not, as yet, become respectable to be equated with the classical languages. Against this background Milton's ambition to write in his native language is commendable. His mind is given to the pursuit of serious learning and writing. He wants to write a poem 'doctrinal to the nation.' Even this poem has to be in English. This may mean losing European fame, but he is prepared for that. He wants to glorify his own language, English.

Milton's first major English poem, *The Nativity Ode*, written in his twenty first year (1629), clearly reveals his profound thinking in terms of devotional poetry. Milton dreams of a golden age, and this concept repeats itself in *Paradise Lost* written towards the close of his life. *The Nativity Ode* with 'its angelology and demonology is indeed a little *Paradise Lost* in anticipation. (Nicolson, 39) The poem is 'more than an ode or a literary hymn,' it shows that 'a poet-prophet is speaking, unfolding a great mystery, and like *Lycidas*, *The Nativity Ode* vaunts beyond its genre into prophecy.' (Beverly) This is indeed Milton's first inspired poem and it strikes a new note in his poetry almost suggesting his belief in himself as a poet-prophet blessed by God. Great poetry is the gift of God, and Milton's Ode foreshadows his consummate artistic excellence as revealed in his three great major poems later.

Milton experiments with English language in his minor poems, the lyrical harmonies, *L'Allegro, Il Penseroso*, recapture the mystic elation, the resurgence of man from a purely physical plane to a life divine. In *Comus* Milton repeats this idea in the opening lines where he says that there are some mortals who 'by due steps' aspire 'and attain divinity.' Milton's firm belief in man being tempted and tested before he is accepted by God finds its affirmation in *Comus*. Through the Elder Brother Milton triumphantly states,

> Virtue may be assailed, but never hurt,
> Surprised by unjust force, but not enthralled.

This firm faith in virtue that is proof against assault is upheld by Milton in all his life. Through the Attendant Spirit Milton expresses his strongly felt belief in virtue that is positive, dynamic and militant. He pleads, 'Love virtue, she alone is free.' Exaltation of virtue as the noblest state in life is typical of Milton's idealism. In the last two lines of *Comus* as in the three long poems later, Milton, the master of perfect endings, reiterates his confirmed opinion that virtue will always have the protective hand of God. *Comus* in its day was no doubt praised for its 'doric delicacy' but we now take it as a poem of exaltation from a mundane life towards heavenliness.

In *Lycidas* Milton feels apologetic for plucking 'berries harsh and crude.' The style acquires a masculine vigour. He uses nature as a mourner for the premature death of Edward King, a fellow student of Christ's college, Cambridge. The poem does not reflect much of personal grief in a conventional manner, for Milton mourns not only for Edward King but also for all young men and young women who may die even before their ambitions are fulfilled. The woods and the desert caves, the willows and the hazel copses, all mourn the loss of Lycidas. Milton observes that true poetry can be judged only by the 'all-judging Jove.' He associates himself with Edward King as a poet and he says it is 'no plant that grows on mortal soil/ Nor on glistering foil.' The poem closes with the setting of the sun and the shepherd twitching his 'mantle blue' so that he may go to 'fresh woods and pastures new.' 'Tomorrow to fresh woods and pastures new' may suggest some change in Milton's habitation or it may cherish a new hope and a new faith in a regenerated world.

Milton's Italian tour gives him the confidence to write a national epic, an *Arthuriad,* but he gets involved in prose pamphleteering. So he experiments with English language by trying various styles of writing. His prose pamphlets reflect his rhetorical skill, presumably reminding him of his Cambridge days, when he had to participate in the prolusions presenting both sides of the arguments. Especially *Areopagitica* and *On Education* reflect his original thinking, clear argumentation and vigorous expression. His pamphlet *Tenure of Kings and Magistrates* with its ardent plea for a Republic immediately brings him an offer from the Commonwealth as Secretary for Foreign Tongues in 1649. As Latin Secretary for 11 years, 1649-60, Milton had to write two *Defences* of the English people in Latin. They brought him European fame and established him as one of the leading persons in the Commonwealth. He thought he was serving a nation 'blessed by God,' but to his dismay and disillusionment he found the nation opting for monarchy in 1660. The great champion of individual liberty and freedom of the nation could only see the restoration of monarchy as an abject surrender to tyranny. He had no faith in the hereditary or divine right theory of kingship.

Restoration of monarchy in 1660 gave him the opportunity to be away from the din and bustle of public duties and responsibilities. He could think of his literary project of writing a great poem, preferably an epic, comparable to the epics of Homer and Virgil. But he could no longer write a national epic for the nation had disappointed him. He had to take up a theme unattempted before, of man's relationship with God. But this is mostly based on his felt religious experience. He could see God's benevolent hand, his unbounded grace, saving him from hanging, but he could not understand why God had allowed the nation to dwindle into an unbecoming thraldom. So he had to bring 'God's Englishmen' back to their fold and explain to them the mysterious, but just ways of God.

This epic, *Paradise Lost*, written towards the close

of Milton's life is 'an adventurous song' that soars aloft 'with no middle flight' Milton's rich experience of life, his wide scholarship, his newly acquired spiritual enlightenment with its understanding of God's ways, all these give to the great poem a unique grandeur and sublimity. Milton's solemn purpose is to 'assert Eternal Providence/And justify the ways of god to men.' No other poet has ever ventured to explain God's ways to the level of human understanding. In the Indian epic, the *Mahabharata*, God himself explains the various methods whereby humanity can attain perfection. Lord Krishna reveals his Viswarupa to Arjuna on the battlefield and explains,

> I am the essence of waters,
> The shining of the sun and the moon,
> Om in all Vedas
> The word that is God. (Gita)

Milton's God reveals himself that he is all alone

> From all eternity, for none I know
> Second to me or like, equal much less.

Raphael expresses the almightiness of God while explaining to Adam that there is one Almighty 'from whom/All things proceed, and up to him return.' In Book III of *Paradise Lost* God elaborately explains Man's relationship with Him. Milton adopts a new style that may appeal to man's sense of reasoning. He makes God say that He has created Adam and Eve free,

> and free they must remain,
> Till they enthrall themselves.

God poses the question,

> So will fall
> He and his faithless progeny. Whose fault?
> Whose but his own.

Milton's God talks like a clever logician trying to convince his listeners that whatever he does, is just and reasonable. That is Milton's experience of justice in God's ways. The Indian epic, the *Mahabharata* and *Paradise Lost* discuss this problem of man's relationship with God using a language that can reasonably be understood by the readers. Both the epics belong to sacred literature where god is introduced as a speaking character. God is made to speak in a language that human intelligence can comprehend. Both the epics follow the tradition of including supernatural agents 'who operate at least partly under human laws.' (Leland, 140) Milton is conversant with the doctrine of accommodation whereby God is brought to the level of human understanding.

This is one kind of argumentative poetic style that Milton adopts in Book III. Book II presents the speeches of the debates in a clever, sophisticated manner. Moloch's forthright statement, 'My sentence is for open war' is followed by Belial's circuitous speech advocating peace, which is nothing but 'ignoble ease and peaceful sloth.' We feel as though we are in a parliamentary session. Milton's grand style mostly figures in Book I where Satan speaks in a heroic vein and expresses sentiments of universal appeal. He proudly utters,

> What though the field be lost?
> All is not lost, the unconquerable will,
> And study of revenge, immortal hate,

And courage never to submit or yield.

Heroic in spirit, Satan defies defeat and proclaims his unyielding courage never to submit to God. Love of liberty is his creed. Critics feel that apparently Milton expresses his love of liberty through this marvellous statement of heroic courage. But Milton slyly introduces a line that in a way cancels the pompous oratory of Satan. All his determination to fight again with God is only for taking revenge and expressing immortal hatred. Revenge and hatred can never be a part of glorification. Especially in Book I Milton introduces a large number of epic similes bringing his epic on a par with the epics of Homer and Virgil. Book IV is lyrical, Book IX is dramatic in style. So Milton has a stupendous task in introducing various styles suited to the occasion in his grand epic.

Peculiarly enough in the first half of this century there has been a vigorous attempt by anti-Miltonists for the dislodgement of Milton. It starts with Ezra Pound and T.S. Eliot. Pound censures Milton's diction and syntax and he finds Milton's verse uninspiring. To Eliot, Milton is thoroughly unsatisfactory 'either from the moralist's point of view, or from the theologian's point of view.' This denigration of Milton is followed by Herbert Read, Middleton Murry and several other anti-Miltonists. F.R. Leavis comments that Milton's dislodgement after his two centuries of predominance, 'was effected with remarkably little fuss.' (42) To him Milton's grand style is monotonous and mechanical, 'as mechanical as bricklaying.' The Miltonists like C.S. Lewis, Tillyard, Hanford, Douglas Bush and several other scholars and teachers champion the cause of Milton's grand style.

C.S.Lewis maintains that Milton's 'ritual style' is the style proper to 'a secondary epic.' E.M.W. Tillyard observes, 'It was one of the fundamental principles of Renaissance and neo-classic criticism that different literary styles were appropriate to different literary forms.' (119) Helen Derbyshire affirms that 'Milton constantly mingled his native English with sonorous Latin.' Wrenn demonstrates the 'astonishing sensitivity' of Milton's verse to the minutest problems of language. Wright supports Milton's language as being based 'on common English, on the current educated speech of his time.' Ricks stoutly upholds the view that 'the grand style admirably fulfilled Leavis's ideal of being sensitive and subtle.' All this vehement vindication of Milton's language produces the desired effect, the rehabilitation of Milton. 'The fact that Milton has triumphantly withheld the modern on-slaught on almost every aspect of his work is a more convincing guarantee of his greatness than the formal reverence accorded to his work by the Victorian critics.' (Murray, 10)

To a discerning reader Milton's style is neither mechanical, nor uninspiring. Milton's style is often praised for its grandeur and sublimity. In *Paradise Lost* we have the happy blending of these various styles artistically rendered. Satan who speaks in a pompous manner in Book I also uses common expressions. For instance in Book IV he tells Gabriel,

> Not to know me argues yourself unknown,
> The lowest of your throng, or if you know,
> Why ask you, and superfluous begin
> Your message, like to end as much in vain?

This is simple enough, but the implied contempt of Satan for Gabriel is also vividly portrayed.

Adam's descriptive account of the spousal in Book VIII with all its romantic idealization of love is superb. Adam tells Raphael,

> To the nuptial bower
> I led her blushing like the morn; all Heaven,
> And happy constellations on that hour
> Shed their selectest influence; the Earth
> Gave signs of gratulation, and each hill;
> Joyous the birds, fresh gales and gentle airs
> Whispered it to the woods, and from their wings
> Flung rose, flung odours from the spicy shrub,
> Disporting, till the amorous bird of night
> Sung spousal, and bid haste the evening star
> On his hill top, to light the bridal lamp.

A glorious scene indeed where Earth feels gratified, birds feel happy, the rose flower dances in ecstasy, and the nightingale gives the nuptial song and bids the evening star to light the bridal lamp. Association of man with nature is typical of the romantic poetry of the early nineteenth century. This passage anticipates Wordsworthian descriptive accounts of nature's glory. We tend to accept Macaulay's view that 'Milton's poetry acts like an incantation and the words are the words of enchantment.' (Smith, 66)

Passages of this type do not tire us. We can appreciate the artist in Milton giving aesthetic pleasure to his readers. On the whole, as Milton states in the opening lines of Book VII, the epic is inspirational poetry, for Urania dictates while he slumbers, and governs his song for a 'fit audience, though few.' Especially the perfect endings Milton chooses to give to these three poems of righteousness and justice make us admire the inspirational poetry that Milton has given to the literary world. The last two lines in *Paradise Lost*,

> Then hand in hand with wandering steps and slow
> Through Eden took their solitary way.

are significant. 'Hand in hand' expresses comradeship, 'wandering steps and slow' indicates the lingering longing for Paradise and finally the 'solitary way' produces the necessary sympathy for the first Man and first Woman. The epic ends on a philosophical calm. Adam and Eve leave paradise in peace.

Similarly after the tempestuous incidents in *Samson Agonistes*, Milton through the Chorus quickly endorses the glorious truth,

> All is best, though we oft doubt,
> What the unsearchable dispose
> Of highest wisdom brings about;

that God comes to the rescue of his devoted servants quite unexpectedly as it has happened to his faithful champion Samson in the hour of triumph.

In *Paradise Regained* we find the Son of God exposed to trials and temptations of all types by Satan. After resisting all those temptations, and after vanquishing Satan, the Son of God unobserved 'Home to his mother's house private returned' so that he may work for the well being of the people.

Milton's epic similes are glorious for he chooses them from Greek mythology, scriptural accounts and travelogues of his time. Even though he does not hold Greek myths in great respect he uses them in order to give to his epic an antiquity. At the same time the seventeenth century reader is familiar with these myths. So the similes based on Greek myths serve the double purpose of making the epic at once remote and familiar. Scripture is something realistic to his age. So by using this material Milton gives to his epic an authenticity and realism. The similes based on travel accounts give to the epic a certain contemporaneity much appreciated by the seventeenth century reader. These long tailed similes also exhibit the vast and varied knowledge of the poet-prophet, Milton. We may consider one such epic simile exhibiting Milton's wide scholarship and profound knowledge. Satan is described in Book I spreading himself 'long and large' on the liquid fire. In bulk he is as huge

> As whom the Fables name of monstrous size,
> Titanian or Earth born, that warr'd on Jove,
> Briareos or Typhon, whom the den
> By ancient Tarsus held, or that sea-beast
> Leviathan, which God of all his works,
> Created hugest that swim the ocean stream.
> Him haply slumbering on the Norway foam,
> The pilot of some small night-foundered skiff,
> Deeming some island, oft, as seamen tell,
> With fixed anchor in the scaly rind,
> Moors by his side under the lee, while night
> Invests the sea, and wished morn delays.
>
> (Bk. I, ll. 197-208)

Satan is like Titan or Briareos or Typhon, all giants 'whom the Fables name of monstrous size.' These references to Greek mythology would have signified to the readers of Milton's day huge proportions and vast dimensions of length, breadth and height. Immeasurable and ponderous Satan could be. Milton adds another comparison likening Satan to the 'leviathan' or Sea monster or 'Rahab' as the Old Testament refers to its defeat once at the time of creation and is to be destroyed or in the metaphor of the sea serpents, 'hooked and landed on the day of judgment.' Milton's imagination also brings into this picture the stories of seamen stating how the whale is mistaken for an island. Seamen settle on it on stormy days and it takes them into the interior of the sea once they start cooking and stirring fires on its back. All these travel accounts have contemporaneous interest. This technique of imparting antiquity, authenticity and contemporaneity to his epic through similes is successfully followed by Milton, thereby exhibiting his superb mastery over English language, Greek mythology, scriptural accounts and travelogues of his day.

Equally amazing are the planes of contrast introduced by Milton with his prophetic vision in the epic structure. This is something unique and Milton manages to give a colourful picture to the movement in the epic by contrasting one picture with the other. The first two books in the epic deal with Hell, signifying darkness, chaos and ugliness. Books III and IV are given to Heaven and Paradise. Celestial glory and paradisal bliss are contrasted with perpetual darkness that prevails in Hell. Hell is 'the gloomy deep,' 'mournful gloom,' 'vast illimitable ocean of darkness,' 'confusion worse confounded.' All these give a negative picture, whereas Heaven and Paradise abound in an 'unlimited cascade of light.' Heaven is described as 'a delectable garden or landscape.' Darkness and light are images of spiritual vacuum and spiritual enlightenment. Incidentally the light-darkness imagery repeats itself in *Paradise Lost* where Christ as the source of light is in conflict with Satan as the power of darkness.

In the first episode consisting of four books, Books V, VI, VII and VIII, the first two books deal with warfare in Heaven. Destruction and ruin figure in the first two books of the episode, the latter two books, Books VII and VIII describe the creation of the universe. The Almighty says, 'let there be light' and there is light. On the sixth day Man is created in the image of God. Destruction in the first two books of the episode is followed by creation.

Books IX and X are mostly domestic scenes dealing with Adam and Eve. Book IX starting with a slight domestic quarrel concludes on the fall of Man and Woman. Book X starts with recrimination, Adam and Eve finding fault with each other, but ends on a note of reconciliation. We see a world of difference between the prelapsarian and postlapsarian state of Adam and Eve. Book IV presents them in 'naked majesty' as lords supreme, but by Book X they are disglorified.

In the last episode Adam and Eve get a peep into the future of mankind. Book XI shows the gradual degeneracy of man, but Book XII describes the regeneration and recreation of mankind, leading finally to the birth of the Messiah.

The technique adopted by Milton in *Paradise Lost* is to familiarize the unfamiliar and this is something unattempted before. Manipulation of this grand material in *Paradise Lost* through varied forms of style, dramatic and narrative, simple and grand is the most significant aspect of this great poem. Mere accumulation of words and phrases, however splendid, can never produce a major epic like *Paradise Lost*. The thought content, the imaginative reconstruction of his own personal experiences, all these reveal that 'any supreme work of art is the product always of a great imagination, the echo of a lofty mind or of a soul possessing some kind of greatness.' (Smith, 64)

It is also felt that the rich 'verbal music' in *Paradise Lost* is due to Milton's possession of 'something of the power of the magicians and exorcists and wizards, who by the rhythmic collocation of wonder-working sounds appeal . . . to the deep and obscure experience of our nature.' (Smith, 65) In view of all these innovative, daring experiments that Milton makes in his grand epic, it is meaningless to think that its style is mechanical or uninspiring. In fact a single passage in *Paradise Lost* is like 'a mosaic of various styles, in keeping with the various characters and situations.' (Bush, VI: 78) Especially when the epic embraces the whole history and destiny of Man, it is almost an imperative to use a style appropriate for the occasion. It is also true that 'the use of blank verse for a heroic poem was in itself a bold innovation . . . and the blank verse of *Paradise Lost* in keeping with the style, creates a new world of expressive rhythm.' (Bush, VI: 79) Unlike the varied and vivid styles in *Paradise Lost*, in *Paradise Regained* the poetic style is mostly refined and its imagery is pervasive. In *Samson Agonistes*, Milton uses the dramatic style. So Milton's use of his native language amply demonstrates and reveals a new world of resources. Even the words of Latin origin were quite familiar to the seventeenth century reader. Shakespeare and the Bible happen to be the English influences on Milton's language.

English language becomes richer and nobler through

Milton's grand style and he makes it as respectable as the classical languages of his day. The blind poet-prophet confers on his native language a richness, an exuberance and a grandeur, making it a world language. Milton is 'world great not because he is world-wide, but because he is world deep.' (Smith, 70) After he had European fame by his *Defence of the English People* in Latin he could have written his epic in Latin. But he decided to glorify his native language. In fact 'no poet ever wrought with such increasing care to give the utmost dignity to the English language,' (Hutchinson, 192) as Milton did. In *The Reason of Church Government*, Milton says that he has applied himself to the resolution 'to fix all the industry and art I could write to the adorning of my native tongue . . . to be an interpreter and relater of the best and sagest things among my own citizens throughout this island, in the mother dialect,' so that he may do for England 'what the greatest and choicest wit of Athens, Rome or modern Italy, and those of Hebrews of old, did for their country.' Milton, the blind poet-prophet, soars aloft and sustains his flight with incredible tenacity and determination.

The Last Elizabethan

Milton is the last Elizabethan who has inherited not only its culture but also its spirit of adventure and exploration. In fact 'he is the only poet of his age who has not forgotten the sublime adventures of the previous century.' (*TLS*) Most probably Milton's interest in Geography even as a student may have kindled in him the desire to see other countries and have an idea of their culture. To him the study of Geography is both profitable and delightful. He has a fondness for maps and 'his imagination was easily kindled by thoughts of different countries abroad over the globe, each with its own geographical features and social customs.' (Daiches, 18) Mercator's Atlas, the first to be published in England in 1636, must have roused in him the curiosity to see other countries and be acquainted with their cultures. It is said that Milton's favourite geographer was Peter Heylyn 'whose *Cosmo-graphie* had been printed in 1652, 1657 and 1660. It was precisely the kind of digest that the poet would be apt to resort to in blindness.' (Cawley, 124) The next geographer in importance for Milton could be Samuel Purchas. A third favourite for the poet was George Sandys. Milton may have liked the maps of his time for 'the elaborate decorations the artists indulge in, filling the spaces representing lands and seas that they do not know with detail out of their fertile imagination.'

(Cawley, 124) Milton uses his geographical knowledge mostly in introducing epic similes in his epic, *Paradise Lost*.

The epic simile describing the various kingdoms of the world by Michael in Book XI, *Paradise Lost* is one such instance of Milton's use of geographical knowledge. Michael shows to Adam through visions the most illustrious kingdoms of the world. Michael takes Adam to the top of a hill so that his

> Eye might there command wherever stood
> City of old or modern fame, the seat
> Of mightiest empire, from the destined walls
> Of Cambalu, seat of Cathaian Can
> And Samarchand by Oxus, Temir's throne,
> To Panquin of Sinaean kings, and thence
> To Agra and Lahor of Great Mogul
> Down to the goden Chersonese. (ll. 385-92)

This lengthy account runs on from line 385 to line 411 in Book XI.

To the readers of his age these names would have signified pomp and luxury, fabulous wealth and fantastic delights. The Asian kingdoms are arranged according to an elaborately centralized pattern. Later the African continent figures. It is remarkable that Milton should give to the Seventeenth Century reader an idea of the various kingdoms of his age. Equally fascinating is the passage in Book III of *Paradise Regained* where Satan tries to tempt the Son of God with kingdoms to be conquered by him. In this passage, ll. 269-321, Satan describes vividly high towered huge cities and mighty empires with the vicious idea of tempting the Saviour. The geographical description of the eastern countries is no doubt poetical.

Partly based on this quest for new lands and new cultures Milton embarks on his Italian journey in 1638. Even after seven years' study at Cambridge, six years' study on his own in Hammersmith and Horton, Milton is still eager to equip his mind with knowledge. His Italian tour reflects his ambition to see new countries so that his great poem will be something unique and unattempted. He thinks that his preparation for writing an immortal epic is not yet adequate.

Milton is helped by introductions from persons of high rank on his onward journey to Italy. He is received in France and Italy with great courtesy. In Paris Lord Scudamore, the ambassador from England, receives him with warmth and sends him with a card of introduction to the great Dutch scholar, Hugo Grotius, at that time ambassador from the Queen of Sweden. This association with Grotius is one of the great influences on Milton for he comes to know of the Indian epics through him. Grotius had knowledge of the Indian epics, especially the *Ramayana*. The *Ramayana* was translated into Russian and other East European languages in the fourteenth century itself.

At Florence Milton receives a friendly welcome from its men of letters. Florence becomes memorable to Milton for he sees Galileo in his seventy fifth year, blind and living under house arrest on the left bank of Arno. Milton describes him as a prisoner to the Inquisition as he happens to think in astronomy differently from the Franciscan and Dominican friars. Milton refers to Galileo very touchingly in Book I of *Paradise Lost* as 'the Tuscan artist' who views the moon's orb through the 'optic glass' at evening from the 'the top of Fesole/ Or in Valdarno.' There are two more references to Galileo in

Books III and V of the epic. Astronomy is one of the subjects very dear to Milton and we can appreciate his reverence to his contemporary astronomer Galileo.

Milton's stay in Rome is equally fruitful. He is invited to a grand musical entertainment at the palace of Cardinal Francesco Barberini. After two months Milton visits Naples where he is introduced to Giovanni Battista Manso, a nobleman of distinguished rank and patron of the illustrious poet Tasso. Manso becomes friendly with Milton and shows him special regard in conducting him round the city. More than once Manso visits Milton at his lodgings.

Milton holds his own views on religion without offence to others or his own conscience. He declares his faith without any reserve or fear even on his second visit to Rome. Milton plans to go to Sicily and Greece also, but he hears that England is about to enter a civil war. So he cuts short his tour and returns to England after fifteen months even though he should have stayed abroad for two years according to his original plan. The Italian journey is an education by itself and he becomes confident to write a great poem 'doctrinal to the nation.'

More than the Italian tour and the wide knowledge he gains, Milton's interest in the East must have been cultivated by him in those six years, 1632-38, while he was reading on his own, books of travel. The East India company was started and the early English travellers were giving fascinating accounts of India, its wealth and riches. In those years Milton would have studied Sir Thomas Roe's *Embassy*, Richard Hakluyt's *Principal Navigations*, *Purchas, His Pilgrimes* and several other travelogues of his day. Later as Secretary for Foreign Tongues in the Commonwealth for eleven years, 1649-

60, he would have been acquainted with some aspects of Indian life and culture.

The Miltons were city merchants who frequently came into contact with the members of the East India Company. Oliver Cromwell granted a charter to the East India Company in 1657. Thomas Stephen, the first Englishman to come to India by the Cape of Good Hope, stayed in Goa from 1579 to 1619 propagating Christianity. His letters to his father, a city merchant in London, gave a good account of the Indian epics and culture. He learnt Marathi and Sanskrit and wrote the *Christian Purana* in Marathi, dealing with the overthrow of Satan and establishment of Christ's kingdom. Another early English traveller Ralph Fitch who lived in India from 1588-1591 was very popular and his observations about India figured in *Purchas, His Pilgrimes.* They created a wide and varied interest and curiosity in the minds of the Englishmen of his day. Veiled references were made to Fitch in the plays of Shakespeare and other literary writers of his age. Similarly the reports of Hawkins, resident ambassador in the court of Jahangir from 1608-13, and of Sir Thomas Roe, the first ambassador from England in the court of Jahangir from 1613 to 15, referred to the opulence, splendour and magnificence of the Moghul court. Especially Sir Thomas Roe's account of oriental pomp as given in the *Embassy* must have fascinated Milton. In the opening lines of Book II of *Paradise Lost* we have the glorious picture of Satan elevated to the position of an emperor with all the glittering show of oriental monarchs. Milton describes the coronation of Satan as the monarch of Hell.

High on a throne of royal state, which far

Outshone the wealth of Ormuz and of Ind,
Or where the gorgeous East with richest hand
Showers on the kings barbaric pearl and gold,
Satan exalted sat, by merit raised
To that bad eminence.

In this comparison one can find the echoes of Sir Thomas Roe's narrative of his first audience with the emperor Jahangir. The splendour of the Moghul court as given by Roe is recaptured in Milton's lines. The oriental pomp, its riches and wealth, its ostentatious practice of showering 'pearl and gold' on the kings must have excited the imagination of the poet and captivated his mind. Sir Thomas Roe describes, 'in the inner court he [Jahangir] sat high in a gallery that went round, with a canopy over him, and a carpet below him in great but barbarous state. To describe it rightly, it was like a great stage, and the Prince sat above as the mock kings do there.' (Purchas, 324)

Milton read the travelogues for profit and pleasure as a young man and he must have 'obviously read to good purpose Haklyut and Purchas and other contemporary travel books like the *Embassy* of Sir Thomas Roe.' (Rawlinson) His memory must have been terrific as he uses all this material in his old age in his great epic, *Paradise Lost* with accuracy and precision.

Especially in his descriptions Milton shows his intimate acquaintance with India. Satan's journey in hell is paralleled with the fleet of ships moving from Bengala, Ternate and Tidore. Satan's odd negotiations with the tempestuous waves of the vast illimitable ocean of darkness, moving to the right, to the left, to the top and to the bottom are likened to the movements of the ships sailing from Bengala. Ternate and Tidore figure very much at that time in the records of the East India Company. In 1579 Drake touched Ternate and 'was believed to have made a treaty with the island's king—facts which many years later fortified the English East India Company to claim [very plainly] prior rights of discovery and treaty as against the monopolizing Dutch.' (*TLS*) Milton describes,

> As when far off at sea a fleet descried
> Hangs in the clouds, by equinoctial winds
> Close sailing from Bengala, or the isles
> Of Ternate and Tidore; whence merchants bring
> Their spicy drugs; they on the trading flood,
> Through the wide Ethiopian to the Cape
> Ply stemming nightly towards the Pole. So seemed
> Far off the flying fiend. (Bk. II, ll. 636-43)

In this passage Milton gives many interesting details. Reference is made to the new route, Cape of Good Hope and the fleet of ships coming from the east with spices. Bengala becomes the centre for coastal trade after the devastating famine in India in 1638. To the readers of Milton's day, Bengala, Ternate and Tidore, Ethiopia would have been places of live interest. Bengala 'is no erudite allusion to a region held marvellous because unknown, dragged in to add opulence to the rhythm and suggestion to the meaning, but a fact as relevant as Ternate and Tidore themselves.' (*TLS*) Bengala occupies a central position for trade and commerce at that time in India.

Equally significant is the picture that Milton gives of Satan's journey to Paradise. Milton's descriptive account showing how the ships move slowly near Mozambic so that they can have the benefit of the sweet fragrance of the winds blowing near the coast, is precise, accurate and fascinating. Milton gives a true picture of the scene,

> As when to them who sail
> Beyond the Cape of Hope, and now are past
> Mozambic, oft at sea northeast winds blow
> Sabean odours from the spicy shore
> Of Araby the Blest, with such delay
> Well pleased they slack their course, and many a league
> Cheered with the grateful smell old Ocean smiles.
> (Bk. IV, ll. 159-65)

Milton likens Satan's journey to one who sails beyond the Cape, past Mozambic and reaches the spicy shore of 'Araby the Blest' there to linger and enjoy the sweet fragrance coming from the winds. Milton is aware of the new route of circumnavigation through the Cape of Good Hope and the ships moving slowly by the Arabian coast so as to enjoy the Sabean odours. Naturally all this material is culled from the books of travel at that time.

Again we have the descriptive account of Satan's journey with particular reference to the eastern regions. In Book III as Milton describes Satan's entrance into Paradise, he says that he is like a vulture,

> on Imaus bred,
> Whose snowy ridge the roving Tartar bounds
> Dislodging from a region scarce of prey
> To gorge the flesh of lambs or yeanling kids
> On hills where flocks are fed, flies towards the springs
> Of Ganges or Hydaspes, Indian streams; (ll. 431-36)

Milton refers to Satan's journey mostly in terms of the oriental background. Both the Indian rivers, the Ganges and the Jhelum (Hydaspes) have their springs in the Himalayas. Satan moves from the Himalayas, from the Tibet region to the barren plains of Sericana, where the Chinese drive 'with sails and wind their cany wagons light.'

Satan driven out of Paradise by Gabriel by the end of Book IV, waits for a suitable opportunity to enter Paradise again. Of the seven days during which Satan goes round and round the earth, three are spent in moving from east to west on the equatorial line; four in moving from pole to pole, from north to south and back. Milton's profound knowledge of the east and of India is again displayed when he describes Satan's movement in Book IX,

> sea he had searched and land
> From Eden over Pontus, and the pool
> Maeotis, up beyond the river Ob;
> Downward as far antarctic; and in length
> West from Orontes to the ocean barred
> At Darien, thence to the land where flows
> Ganges and Indus; thus the orb he roamed
> With narrow search; (ll 76-83)

The precision with which Milton describes Satan's wanderings, astronomically as well as geographically is superb. Along the equatorial line Satan travels westward from the Syrian river Orontes to the Isthumus of Darien, continues further on round to India, passes first the Ganges and then the Indus. The order of passing from Ganges to Indus is a remarkable sign of Milton's accurate knowledge of the east, especially of India. It is significant that even the direction in which the rivers flow is given by Milton with precision.

Paradise Lost is full of these descriptive accounts that must have fascinated the seventeenth century reader immensely. To the readers of the present age they are full of amazing curiosity and wonder for they exhibit the blind poet's spirit of adventure and love of other countries and other cultures like a typical Elizabethan. Milton's description of the Indians in *Paradise Regained* is again based on a penetrating vision of the east. In *Paradise Regained* in the process of tempting the Saviour, Satan follows the technique of mentioning Rome and other cities of the world and brings him to India. Satan shows the moving picture to the Son of God,

> From India and the golden Chersonese,
> And utmost isle Taprobane
> Dusk faces with silken turbans wreathed.
>
> (Bk. IV, ll. 74-76)

Aptly Milton presents the exotic, colourful picture of the Indians of that age, characteristically with 'dusk faces' and 'silk turbans.'

Nor does Milton fail to refer to the rich vegetation in India. The plenteous aspect revealed through Nature's bounty is given in *Paradise Lost* when Eve prepares the most delicious fare for Raphael, culled:

> from each tender stalk
> Wherever Earth all-bearing Mother yields
> In India east or west or middle shore
> In Pontus or the Panic coast. (Bk. V, ll. 337-40)

Milton pays a glowing tribute to Mother Earth in India and elsewhere. India figures in Milton's mind as a land of fruitfulness noted for its rich vegetation. Milton revels in these gorgeous accounts of the east, especially of India. There are several references to distant lands and cities, Ormuz and Ind, Agra and Lahore, Damasco, Morocco and Trebisond, Congo and Angola—all these would have given to the readers of his age the picture of a world as fascinating as El Dorado itself.

But the most elaborate and delightful picture Milton gives of the fig tree, the banyan tree, in Book IX, is something extraordinary and unattempted by any other poet of the east or the west. Even in Indian poetry we do not get such a vivid, colourful imaginative picture of a banyan tree, not one tree but a synod of trees, so common in Malabar and Deccan. After the fall, Adam and Eve desperately try to cover their naked bodies. In the prelapsarian state ignorance was bliss. But now in the postlapsarian state knowledge becomes irksome for they realise that they are naked. Milton is at his best in making the pair cover their bodies with fig leaves. In Book IX we have the imaginative reconstruction of the scene. Adam and Eve go

> Into the thickest wood, there they soon choose
> The fig tree, not that kind for fruit renowned,
> But such as at this day to Indians known
> In Malabar or Decan spreads her arms,
> Branching so broad and long, that in the ground
> The blended twigs take root and daughters grow
> About the mother-tree, a pillared shade
> High overarched, and echoing walks between;
> There oft the Indian herdsman shunning heat
> Shelters in cool, and tends his pasturing herds
> At loopholes cut through thickest shade, these leaves
> They gathered. (ll. 1100-11)

To an Indian even to this day the banyan tree with its branches spread over a large area of ground, is a familiar sight. These trees grow plenteously especially in the south, in Malabar and Deccan, as Milton describes. Milton brings into this picture of the banyan tree vivid imagination and faithful accumulation of details ultimately making it authentic. The mother tree is supported by the twigs, its daughters. The banyan tree like the monumental oak tree stands for ages and ages as a sentinel of humanity. The Indian herdsmen and shepherds protecting themselves from the heat sit under the shade of the tree with its clustering branches. The sylvan atmosphere, the summer heat and the cool refreshing shade of the tree can easily be imagined through this detailed, picturesque account. Milton also refers to the loopholes through which the herdsmen watch their cattle grazing nearby. It is of great significance that Milton could give such an elaborate picture of the tree so faithfully as if he has seen it personally and enjoyed the sheltering shade.

One is inclined to think that Milton may have received useful and purposeful information from many of the animated talks he had with some of the factors of the East India Company. Methwold, the scholarly President of Surat factory in India from 1633-1639, had been closely connected with Milton. Even after his retirement Methwold acted as committee and deputy chairman of the East India Company in London from 1639 till his death in 1653. It is likely that Milton may have received a vast and realistic information from India-returned persons like Methwold. Even then it is difficult to give so many details about the banyan tree making the whole description picturesque. Milton pointedly clarifies that the fig tree he is describing is not the fruit bearing fig tree, but a tree that grows in India, especially in the south, and is noted for its leaves and shade.

Milton's knowledge of India is not particularly restricted to its geographical conditions. He seems to be acquainted with the thought content of the Indian epics for his mind with its catholicity of outlook is given to the study of the epics written in various languages of the east or the west. It is not surprising therefore that Milton's ethical idealism and his insistence on unswerving loyalty to God have affinity with the philosophical background of the Indian epics. His views conform to the pattern of the Indian doctrine of *prapatti*, self-surrender, as illustrated in the two Indian epics. The *Ramayana* and the *Mahabharata* insist on man's willing submission to God. The three epics show the reasonableness of God's actions.

Milton upholds the view that God exposes even his faithful devotees to trials and temptations before he accepts them. Milton's God assures the angels in Heaven that

> To prayer, repentance, and obedience due,
> Though but endeavoured with sincere intent,
> Mine ear shall not be slow, mine eye not shut.
>
> (*P.L.*, Book III, ll. 191-93)

Milton's view that 'a good temptation is that whereby God tempts even the righteous for the purpose of proving them' is typically true of the Indian thought content where God chooses to test his followers before he blesses them. Like Milton's God, Lord Krishna affirms,

Quickly I come
To those who offer me
Every action
Worship me only. (*Gita*)

Milton's ethical idealism and the philosophical background of the two Indian epics come from the same source, Perennial philosophy, that affirms the existence of human incarnation of the Divine Ground, by whose grace the worshipper is helped to achieve his goal. Milton's kaleidoscopic knowledge is essentially of this phenomenal type. Milton, the last Elizabethan, is the innovator of the cross-cultural assimilation of the east and the west, so eloquently propagated in the present day world.

Milton Today

Milton survives today not only as an illustrious poet of an immortal epic, but also as 'one of the greatest' liberators like Luther and Blake in his attempt to break the bonds of guilt, to relieve mankind from the superstition of scarecrow sins.' (Hill, 458) Milton is concerned with the well being of the people. He spends twenty years of his life in fighting for 'the good old cause' of individual liberty and freedom of the country. He thinks in terms of a Commonwealth, a Republic that may give greater freedom to the people. It is a welfare state where people enjoy peace and prosperity. In his fight for political or religious freedom he does not exhibit any personal ambition, 'not even the fevered search for personal salvation' (Hill, 460) that we find in Vaughan or in Bunyan. His prose pamphlet, *To establish a free Commonwealth* published a few weeks before Restoration in 1660 amply illustrates his concern for 'Christ's kingdom, the good society, rather than with personal consolations or reward.' (Hill, 460) In his pamphlet he questions, 'where is the goodly tower of a Commonwealth, which the English boasted they would build to overthrow kings, and be another Rome in the West.' With the restoration of monarchy Milton realizes that his appeal to the people is like a cry in wilderness, like the prophet saying 'O earth, earth, earth' to indicate 'what her perverse inhabitants are deaf to.'

Milton is thoroughly disillusioned with his people. In that mood he can only dream of a kingdom ruled by Christ and his saints, a millennium, a golden age of golden deeds. He relies on his poetic imagination and he beholds a new world order where righteousness prevails, and it will be richer than the political institutions in their generous dispensation of justice. Into this world of ethical idealism Milton takes the reader for illumination and ennoblement. Having failed to realise the establishment of a Commonwealth even after twenty years of struggle and loss of sight, Milton ventures to offer that world through his epic.

We first get a picture of this world of golden deeds in Book III of the epic, as an apocalyptic vision of God himself. God explains to the good angels in Heaven that the Son of God will redeem mankind and will show heavenly love overpowering hellish hate. The world of sin will be destroyed and from its ashes will spring 'New heaven and earth wherein the just shall dwell.' God observes,

> And after all this tribulation long
> See golden days, fruitful of golden deeds
> With joy and love triumphing,

that a new world will be created. In this world godliness, divine love and celestial glory will reign supreme. This beatific vision of a golden age is presented by Milton in Book III itself but he has to substantiate his prophetic utterance through the manipulation of events in the epic. Finally in Book XII Milton triumphantly presents the restoration of the world and the regeneration of mankind. The last two books of *Paradise Lost* 'are Adam's and everyone's books, not theology.' (Patrides, 31) They are no doubt meant for the spiritual enlightenment and purification of Adam, yet they influence everyone into thinking of a recreated world of hope and faith. Even to this day the quest for an ideal world is a reality. 'The evolution of Milton's thought and feeling, the deepening of the spiritual makes him very much our contemporary.' (Barker, 173) By creating Adam with heroic virtue and philosophical calm, and by making him a typical everyman Milton indicates that the last two books of the epic reveal the spiritual experience of every regenerated man. These two books illustrate Milton's avowed aim of asserting 'Eternal providence' and justifying 'the ways of God to men.'

In Book XII Milton first shows to Adam the degenerate condition of religious matters for

> Wolves shall succeed for teachers, grievous wolves,
> Who all the sacred mysteries of heaven
> To their own vile advantages shall turn
> Of lucre and ambition, and the truth
> With superstitions and traditions taint. (ll. 508-12)

and the world goes on unmindful of the injustice done to man by man. This attack reminds us of Milton's *Lycidas* where he comments on the clergymen of his day, who 'creep and intrude and climb into the fold,' not knowing even the fundamentals of their profession.

Michael also refers to the inequalities and the injustices that are perpetrated without any moral compunction or fear. He tells Adam,

> so shall the world go on,

To good malignant, to bad men benign
Under her own weight groaning, till the day
Appear of respiration to the just
And vengeance to the wicked at return
Of him so lately pronounced to the aid.
(Bk. XII, ll. 537-42)

While dreaming of a millennium Milton does not fail to present the deplorable state of human existence before it is redeemed and recreated by the coming of Christ in the human form. Michael refers to the second coming of Christ when he will establish the world of justice and righteousness. The perverted world of Satan with all its diabolical urges will be dissolved and

From the conflagrant mass, purged and refined,
New heavens, new earth, ages of endless date
Founded in righteousness and peace and love,
To bring forth fruits, joy and eternal bliss
(Bk. XII, ll. 548-51)

a new world of justice will be created.

This is the glorious picture of the golden age that Milton dreams of. This heaven upon earth is based on righteousness, 'dharma,' peace and love. This divinely ordained world will bring forth joy and eternal bliss. Milton's view of a golden age is like the reassuring promise of Lord Krishna to Arjuna on the battlefield,

In every age I come back
To deliver to holy,
To destroy the sin of the sinner
To establish righteousness. (*Bhagavad Gita*)

Milton's vision of a millennium is an enduring phenomenon for it creates a new hope and a new faith in human existence. Milton reveals in the last two books of the epic, 'his intellect, a revelation of the power of his mind, the greatness of his idea, the continuing tone of nobility with which he pursues his quest to establish the right manner of life and conduct.' (Patrides, 51)

Adam is ennobled through visions and exhortations by Michael. He affirms that he has learnt the lesson of obedience to God and to depend on God's grace only. Adam now understands that God is

> Merciful over all his works, with good
> Still overcoming evil and by small
> Accomplishing great things, by things deemed weak
> Subverting worldly strong, and worldly wise
> By simply meek, that suffering for truth's sake
> Is fortitude to highest victory. (ll. 565-70)

This spiritual exaltation is in conformity with Milton's vision of an ideal world. Michael assures Adam that he has 'attained the sum/ Of wisdom.'

Adam has acquired a 'Paradise within, happier far' than the physical Paradise he has lost. Milton's epic, *Paradise Lost* ends on a note of resurgence with the promise of God's gracious rule of justice. This seems to be the personal experience of Milton, of things to come in an ethical world where the weak and godfearing persons can subvert the worldly strong and worldly wise men. It shows Milton's courage and his solemn faith in the transcendent glory of divine direction, and he is quite convinced that 'suffering for truth's sake/ Is fortitude to highest victory.' Milton's abiding faith in the great values of life makes him like Abdiel faithful 'among the faithless.' To understand the relevance of Milton today we must take into consideration his total political commitment to the nation. The determination to uphold 'what he believes to be right, however complete the apparent defeat of the cause, makes Milton every age's contemporary.' (Hill, 460)

Milton undauntedly takes up the challenging task of writing a poem 'unattempted yet in prose or rhyme' despite his blindness and other disheartening circumstances overpowering him. Milton's heroic virtue, at the personal level, is something to be emulated in every age. The western critics often present him as a typical Englishman. But he transcends the limitations of nationalism.

Milton's epic *Paradise Lost*, like the Indian epics, the *Ramayana* and the *Mahabharata*, belongs to sacred literature written by saintly persons for whom pain and pleasure have no perceptible significance. As Lord Krishna tells Arjuna on the battlefield,

> Pain follows pleasure
> He is not troubled,
> Gain follows loss,
> He is indifferent. (*Gita*)

Such a person is 'Jnani' for he is unmoved by pleasure and pain and is indifferent to worldly entanglements.

In Valmiki's *Ramayana* Rama's concern is to establish Ramarajya, an ideal kingdom where people enjoy peace and harmony. This is Valmiki's prophetic vision of a golden age. The *Ramayana* and *Paradise Lost* do not concentrate on personal salvation or the means for attaining it. The poets are deeply involved in a world of peace and joy to all human beings. They wish to have a heaven upon earth. Both the poets, Milton and Valmiki, dream of a perfect world, a golden age. So the two epics, the *Ramayana* and *Paradise Lost* look like contemporary political treatises. This is one aspect of the two poems, apart from being illustrious epics. The *Mahabharata*, the other Indian epic, gives a complete picture of the religious, political and social conditions of India in that early period. This epic, unlike the other two epics, refers to personal salvation also. In the *Gita* section, the epic vividly describes and preaches the path of deliverance from mundane fetters.

The three epics insist on unswerving loyalty to God. They are epics of righteousness and envisage a golden age of golden deeds. The conflict of good and evil and the ultimate triumph of good forces forms the thematic content of the three epics. Doing duty for its own sake, irrespective of the reward, 'Nishkama karma' is the message that the three epics give. In the *Gita* Lord Krishna refers to such a person, 'He who does the task/Dictated by duty/Caring nothing/For the fruit of the action' as a Yogi.

We cannot possibly say that Milton had a complete knowledge of the Indian epics or their thought content. But his mind is given to a thinking that is universal. Milton with his humanism wants God's work to be done for its own sake, for God chooses his saints and prophets to do his work for humanity. Milton may have been influenced by Puritanism, Cambridge Platonism, Christian Humanism and several other forms of movements at that time. But he remains to be an independent individual with his intellectual fervour and moral sensitiveness.

Even his concept of chastity as virtue that may be assailed but not enthralled is typically Indian. Even to this day Indians view with respect Sita, Savitri and several other women for their essential chastity and purity. Milton explains in his *Apology for Smectymnus* how he has learnt chastity as divinity from Plato and other great thinkers. Milton with his vast reading and knowledge of several epics written in various languages, takes up his epic with a rare and unique mental disposition. Even though he takes a biblical tale for his epic, he imbues it with all the learning he has gained in his life. His thought content, not being orthodox, appeals to every thinking man. Especially to the Indian mind, *Paradise Lost* with its lofty idealism, its perception of man's relationship with God, its insistence on implicit faith in God, and finally its prophetic vision of a golden age, offers a delightful experience of ethical wisdom.

Milton today is relevant not only as a poet of rare excellence, but also as a sublime political prophet of a golden age. Milton becomes 'outmoded only when the millennium arrives.' (Hill, 460) Once the golden age is established he becomes irrelevant, but that seems to be a long enough period. Milton's three long poems, written towards the close of his life, make us realize that

> Just are the ways of God,
> And justifiable to men;
> Unless there be who think not God at all.
>
> (*Samson Agonistes*, ll. 293-95)

Bibliography

Barker, Arthur E., ed. *Modern Essays in Criticism.* Oxford, 1972.

Beverly, Sherry. "Milton's Mystic Nativity," *Milton Quarterly*, vol. 17, 1983.

Broadbent, John, ed. *John Milton, Introduction*. C.U.P., 1973.

Bush, Douglas. *Paradise Lost* in *Milton Encyclopaedia*, vol. 6.

Cawley, Robert R. "Geography and Milton." *Milton Encyclopaedia*, vol. 3.

Daiches, David. *Milton*. Hutchinson, 1957.

Frye, Northrop. "Notes on Tragic Hero," in *Twentieth Century Interpretations of "Samson Agonistes."*

Frye, Ronald Mushat. *Milton's Imagery and Visual Arts*. Princeton University Press, 1978.

Grierson, H.G.C. *Milton and Wordsworth, Poets and Prophets.*

Hill, Christopher. *Milton and the English Revolution*. Faber and Faber, 1977.

Hughes, Merrit. "The Christ of *Paradise Regained* and the Renaissance Tradition," *Studies in Philology*, vol. 35, 1938.

Hunter, William B. *The Descent of Urania, Studies in Milton, 1946-88*. Associated Presses, 1989.

Hutchinson. F.E. *Milton and the English Mind*. English Universities Press, 1946.

Johnson *Life of Milton*, ed. Deighton.

Kermode, Frank. *The Living Milton*. Routledge and Kegan Paul, 1960.

Leavis, F.R. *Revaluations*.

Leland, Ryken. *The Apocalyptic Vision in "Paradise Lost."* Cornell University Press, 1970.

Lewalaski, Barbara. *Milton's Brief Epic*. Methuen, 1966.

______. "*Samson Agonistes* and the Tragedy of the Apocalypse," *PMLA*, vol. 35, no. 5, October 1970.

Lewis, C.S. Preface to *Paradise Lost*.

Miller, Leo. *John Milton and the Oldenburg Safeguard*. Longwonthal Press, 1995.

Murray, Patrick. *Milton, the Modern Phase*.

Nicolson, Margery Hope. *John Milton*. Thames and Hudson, 1964.

Patrides, C.A. *"Paradise Lost" and the Christian Tradition*.

_______. *Approaches to "Paradise Lost."*

_______, ed. *Milton's Epic Poetry*. Penguin, 1967.

Purchas. *His Pilgrims*, vol. IV.

Rajan, B. *"Paradise Lost" and the Seventeenth Century Reader*.

Rawlinson, H.G. "Indian Influence on Western Culture," *JRAS*, 1947.

Sensabaugh, George F. *That Grand Whig, Milton*. Stanford University Press, 1952.

Smith, Logan Pearsall. *Milton and His Modern Critics*.

Stein, Arnold. "The Return of Samson," in *Twentieth Century Interpretations of "Samson Agonistes."*

Taylor, Thomas *Christ's Combat*.

Tillyard, E.M.W. *The Miltonic Setting*.

Tillyard, Phyllis B., ed. *John Milton's Private Correspondence*.

Times Literary Supplement, March 30, 1933. "Ormuz and Amurath."

Waldock, A.J. *"Paradise Lost" and Its Critics*. C.U.P., 1961.

Wolfe, Don M. *Milton and His England*. Princeton: Princeton University Press, 1971.

Woodhouse, A.S.P. "The Possibility of Christian Tragedy," in *Twentieth Century Interpretations of "Samson Agonistes."*

